# AAT

# AQ2016

## Cash and Treasury Management

# EXAM KIT

This Exam Kit supports study for the following AAT qualifications:
AAT Professional Diploma in Accounting – Level 4
AAT Level 4 Diploma in Business Skills
AAT Professional Diploma in Accounting at SCQF Level 8

**British Library Cataloguing-in-Publication Data**

A catalogue record for this book is available from the British Library.

Published by:

Kaplan Publishing UK
Unit 2 The Business Centre
Molly Millar's Lane
Wokingham
Berkshire
RG41 2QZ

ISBN: 978-1-78740-293-5

© Kaplan Financial Limited, 2018

Printed and bound in Great Britain.

# CONTENTS

---

**Features in this exam kit**

In addition to providing a wide ranging bank of real assessment style questions, we have also included in this kit:

- unit-specific information and advice on assessment technique

- our recommended approach to make your revision for this particular subject as effective as possible.

---

You will find a wealth of other resources to help you with your studies on the AAT website:

www.aat.org.uk/

Quality and accuracy are of the utmost importance to us so if you spot an error in any of our products, please send an email to mykaplanreporting@kaplan.com with full details, or follow the link to the feedback form in MyKaplan.

Our Quality Co-ordinator will work with our technical team to verify the error and take action to ensure it is corrected in future editions.

# UNIT-SPECIFIC INFORMATION

## THE EXAM

### FORMAT OF THE ASSESSMENT

The assessment is divided into ten standalone tasks which cover all of the learning outcomes and assessment criteria.

In any one assessment, students may not be assessed on all content, or on the full depth or breadth of a piece of content. The content assessed may change over time to ensure validity of assessment, but all assessment criteria will be tested over time.

The learning outcomes for this unit are as follows:

| | Learning outcome | Weighting |
|---|---|---|
| 1 | Use statistical techniques and financial information to prepare forecasts of cash receipts and payments | 10% |
| 2 | Prepare cash budgets and monitor cash flows within the organisation | 20% |
| 3 | Evaluate the principles of cash management within the context of regulation and government monetary policies | 20% |
| 4 | Evaluate ways of raising finance in accordance with organisational requirements | 25% |
| 5 | Evaluate ways of investing surplus funds within organisational policies | 25% |
| | Total | 100% |

**Time allowed**

2 hours 30 minutes

### PASS MARK

The pass mark for all AAT CBAs is 70%.

 **Always keep your eye on the clock and make sure you attempt all questions!**

## DETAILED SYLLABUS

The detailed syllabus and study guide written by the AAT can be found at:

www.aat.org.uk/

KAPLAN PUBLISHING

# INDEX TO QUESTIONS AND ANSWERS

# EXAM TECHNIQUE

- **Do not skip any of the material** in the syllabus.

- **Read each question** *very* carefully.

- **Double-check your answer** before committing yourself to it.

- Answer **every** question – if you do not know an answer to a multiple choice question or true/false question, you don't lose anything by guessing. Think carefully before you **guess**.

- If you are answering a multiple-choice question, **eliminate first those answers that you know are wrong**. Then choose the most appropriate answer from those that are left.

- **Don't panic** if you realise you've answered a question incorrectly. Getting one question wrong will not mean the difference between passing and failing

## Computer-based assessments – tips

- Do not attempt a CBA until you have **completed all study material** relating to it.

- On the AAT website there is a CBA demonstration. It is **ESSENTIAL** that you attempt this before your real CBA. You will become familiar with how to move around the CBA screens and the way that questions are formatted, increasing your confidence and speed in the actual assessment.

- Be sure you understand how to use the **software** before you start the assessment. If in doubt, ask the assessment centre staff to explain it to you.

- Questions are **displayed on the screen** and answers are entered using keyboard and mouse. At the end of the assessment, you are given a certificate showing the result you have achieved.

- In addition to the traditional multiple-choice question type, CBAs will also contain **other types of questions**, such as number entry questions, drag and drop, true/false, pick lists or drop down menus or hybrids of these.

- In some CBAs you will have to type in written answers.

- You need to be sure you **know how to answer questions** of this type before you sit the assessment, through practice.

KAPLAN PUBLISHING

# KAPLAN'S RECOMMENDED REVISION APPROACH

## QUESTION PRACTICE IS THE KEY TO SUCCESS

Success in professional assessments relies upon you acquiring a firm grasp of the required knowledge at the tuition phase. In order to be able to do the questions, knowledge is essential.

However, the difference between success and failure often hinges on your assessment technique on the day and making the most of the revision phase of your studies.

The **Kaplan textbook** is the starting point, designed to provide the underpinning knowledge to tackle all questions. However, in the revision phase, poring over text books is not the answer.

**Kaplan pocket notes** are designed to help you quickly revise a topic area; however you then need to practise questions. There is a need to progress to assessment style questions as soon as possible, and to tie your assessment technique and technical knowledge together.

**The importance of question practice cannot be over-emphasised.**

The recommended approach below is designed by expert tutors in the field, in conjunction with their knowledge of the examiner and the specimen assessment.

**You need to practise as many questions as possible in the time you have left.**

## OUR AIM

Our aim is to get you to the stage where you can attempt assessment questions confidently, to time, in a closed book environment, with no supplementary help (i.e. to simulate the real assessment experience).

Practising your assessment technique is also vitally important for you to assess your progress and identify areas of weakness that may need more attention in the final run up to the assessment.

In order to achieve this we recognise that initially you may feel the need to practise some questions with open book help.

**Good assessment technique is vital.**

# THE KAPLAN REVISION PLAN

## Stage 1: Assess areas of strengths and weaknesses

Review the key topic listings for this paper

Determine whether or not each area is one with which you are comfortable

Comfortable with the technical content

Not comfortable with the technical content

Read the relevant chapter(s) in Kaplan's Study Text

Attempt the 'Test Your Understanding' questions if unsure of an area

Review the Pocket Notes on this area

## Stage 2: Practice questions

Follow the order of revision of topics as presented in this kit and attempt the questions in the order suggested.

Try to avoid referring to text books and notes and the model answer until you have completed your attempt.

Review your attempt with the model answer and assess how much of the answer you achieved.

## Stage 3: Final pre-assessment revision

We recommend that you **attempt at least one two and a half hour mock assessment** containing a set of previously unseen assessment standard questions.

Attempt the mock CBA online in timed, closed book conditions to simulate the real exam experience.

# Section 1

# PRACTICE QUESTIONS

## CASH AND PROFIT

### TYPES OF CASH FLOW

1    Complete the table by selecting the best description from the list of options below to match the type of cash receipt or cash payment.

| Description | Type of receipt or payment |
|---|---|
| Proceeds from the disposal of non-current assets | |
| Buy new factory | |
| Customer paying their debt | |
| Pay legal fee due to product complaints | |
| Unexpected tax refund | |
| Payment of wages | |
| Pay corporation tax for the year | |
| Payments made to the owners of the business | |

**Options**

1    Capital payment

2    Capital receipts

3    Drawings

4    Exceptional payment

5    Exceptional receipt

6    Regular revenue receipt

7    Regular revenue expense

8    Payment to HM Revenue and Customs

## CASH ADJUSTMENTS

**2** **Statement of Financial Position extract:**

| Balances as at: | 31 October 20X8 | 31 October 20X9 |
|---|---|---|
| | £ | £ |
| Trade receivables | 10,500 | 12,900 |
| Prepayment – rent | 750 | 1,000 |
| Accrual – payroll expenses | 200 | 320 |
| Trade payables | 5,800 | 6,300 |

**Statement of profit or loss extract for the year ended 31 October 20X9**

| | £ | £ |
|---|---|---|
| Revenue | | 300,000 |
| Less: Purchases | | (150,000) |
| Gross profit | | 150,000 |
| Less: Expenses | | |
| Payroll | 22,120 | |
| Rent | 6,000 | |
| Utilities | 10,000 | |
| | | (38,120) |
| | | 111,880 |

(a) Prepare the trade receivables account, showing clearly the cash received from receivables in the year.

Trade receivables

| | £ | | £ |
|---|---|---|---|
| | | | |

(b) Prepare the rent account, showing clearly the amount of cash paid for rent for the year.

Rent

| | £ | | £ |
|---|---|---|---|
| | | | |

(c)   **Prepare the payroll expenses account, showing clearly the cash paid for payroll expenses for the year.**

Payroll expenses

| | £ | | £ |
|---|---|---|---|
| | | | |

(d)   **Prepare the trade payables account, showing clearly the cash paid to the payables in the year.**

Trade payables

| | £ | | £ |
|---|---|---|---|
| | | | |

**3**   The following items were extracted from a company's budget for next month:

| | £ |
|---|---|
| Purchases on credit | 360,000 |
| Expected decrease in inventory during the month | 12,000 |
| Expected increase in trade payables during the month | 15,000 |

**What is the budgeted payment to trade payables for the month?**

A   £333,000

B   £345,000

C   £357,000

D   £375,000

**4**   DY had a balance outstanding on trade receivables at 30 April 20X6 of £70,000. Forecast credit sales for the next six months are £200,000 and customers are expected to return goods with a sales value of £2,000.

Based on past experience, within the next six months DY expects to collect £250,000 cash and to write off as irrecoverable debts 3% of the balance outstanding at 30 April 20X6.

**Calculate DY's forecast trade receivables outstanding at 31 October 20X6.**

**5**   The following items are included in a company's budget for next month:

| | £ |
|---|---|
| Sales on credit | 240,000 |
| Expected increase in inventory next month | 20,000 |
| Expected decrease in trade receivables next month | 12,000 |

**What is the budgeted receipt from trade receivables next month?**

**6** A business disposed of a number of non-current assets.

**Calculate the cash received in each of the following situations.**

(a) A vehicle has been disposed of during the year.

- The original cost of the vehicle was £12,000.
- The accumulated depreciation on the vehicle was £5,250.
- The loss on disposal was £1,750.

**How much cash was received?**

(b) An item of equipment was disposed of during the year.

- The original cost of the equipment was £500.
- It was purchased 3 years ago and depreciation is provided at 20% on a straight line basis.
- There was a gain of £75 from the sale of this equipment.

**How much cash was received?**

(c) A vehicle was part-exchanged for a new one during the year.

- The original cost of the vehicle which was part-exchanged was £12,000.
- The carrying amount of the vehicle which was part-exchanged was £6,144.
- The part exchange would generate a book loss on the old car of £2,644.
- The new vehicle's total cost was £13,500.

**What was the value of the part-exchange and therefore how much cash was spent buying the new vehicle?**

**7** Haul Punt owns a business which caters for weddings and other grand functions. Haul prepares quarterly statements of profit or loss and statements of financial position. These are prepared on an accruals basis.

Haul likes to use the freshest ingredients, so these are mainly purchased when required and therefore very little inventory is maintained. All sales and purchases are made on credit terms.

The statement of profit or loss for Haul's business for the quarter ended June is as follows:

|  | £ | £ |
|---|---|---|
| Revenue |  | 51,000 |
| Less: Purchases |  | (26,000) |
| Gross profit |  | 25,000 |
| Less: Expenses |  |  |
| Wages | 12,900 |  |
| Advertising expenses | 2,010 |  |
| Van expenses | 3,069 |  |
| Van depreciation | 2,567 |  |
|  |  | (20,546) |
|  |  | 4,454 |

Extracts from the statement of financial position at 1 April and 30 June show the following:

| Statement of financial position at | 1 April | 30 June |
|---|---|---|
| | £ | £ |
| Receivables | 3,520 | 12,400 |
| Payables | 400 | 3,004 |
| Accruals – advertising | 1,200 | 800 |
| Prepayments – van expenses | 80 | 110 |

**Calculate the actual business cash receipts and cash payments for the quarter to 30 June.**

| | £ |
|---|---|
| Sales receipts | |
| Purchases payments | |
| Wages paid | |
| Advertising fees paid | |
| Van expenses | |
| Van depreciation | |

**8** The statement of profit or loss for Ben's business for the quarter ended June shows the following:

| | £ |
|---|---|
| Revenue | 351,000 |
| Purchases | 126,000 |
| Wages expense | 32,900 |
| Electricity expenses | 22,010 |
| Van expenses | 23,069 |
| Phone expense | 12,567 |

Extracts from the statements of financial position at 1 April and 30 June show the following:

| Statement of financial position at | 1 April | 30 June |
|---|---|---|
| | £ | f |
| Receivables | 13,520 | 31,000 |
| Payables | 4,400 | 8,000 |
| Accruals – electricity and van | 1,200 | 2,100 |
| Prepayments – phone expenses | 80 | – |

**Calculate the actual business cash receipts and cash payments for the quarter to 30 June.**

| | £ |
|---|---|
| Sales receipts | |
| Purchases payments | |
| Wages paid | |
| Electricity and van expenses paid | |
| Phone expenses | |

**9** S Nynan owns a wedding stationery business and prepares quarterly statements of profit or loss and statements of financial positions. These are prepared on an accruals basis.

Stationery materials are purchased when required and therefore very little inventory is maintained. All sales and purchases are made on credit terms.

The following information has been extracted from the accounting information for S Nynan's business for the quarter ended September:

| | Statement of profit or loss £ | Opening position | | Closing position | |
|---|---|---|---|---|---|
| | | Prepayments £ | Accruals £ | Prepayments £ | Accruals £ |
| Rent | 12,650 | 1,200 | | | 1,200 |
| Office expenses | 6,640 | | 370 | | 441 |
| Printing expenses | 17,118 | 3,655 | | 567 | |

**Calculate the actual business cash payments for the quarter ended September.**

| | £ |
|---|---|
| Rent paid | |
| Office expenses paid | |
| Printing expenses paid | |

**10** Mark Goss started trading on 1 April 20X6. He is a computer technician working for small businesses and all trade is on credit.

Extracts from the statement of profit or loss as at 31 March 20X7:

| | £ |
|---|---|
| Revenue | 29,200 |
| Purchases | 11,200 |
| Rent | 3,600 |
| General expenses | 1,840 |

- On 31 March 20X7, trade receivables owed £3,400.
- On 31 March 20X7, £1,195 was owed to payables for supplies.
- Discounts were received amounting to £1,165.
- The cash paid for rent included a payment of £900 for rent of the premises for the period 1 April 20X7 to 30 June 20X7.
- During May 20X7, a payment of £135 was made for electricity used during the period 1 February 20X7 to 30 April 20X7. Electricity is charged to general expenses.

(a) **Calculate the cash received from receivables for the year ended 31 March 20X7**

(b) **Calculate the cash paid to payables for the year ended 31 March 20X7**

(c) **Calculate the cash paid for rent for the year ended 31 March 20X7**

(d) **Calculate the cash paid for general expenses for the year ended 31 March 20X7**

**11** The following forecast information has been provided for a business for the quarter ending 31 July 20X6:

|  | £ | £ |
|---|---|---|
| Revenue |  | 15,000 |
| Less: Cost of sales |  |  |
| Opening inventory | 1,200 |  |
| Purchases | 2,400 |  |
| Closing inventory | (1,000) |  |
|  |  | (2,600) |
| Gross profit |  | 12,400 |
| Expenses |  | 1,880 |
| Operating profit |  | 10,520 |
| Tax |  | 2,700 |
| Profit after tax |  | 7,820 |

**Additional information**

1 The company believes that 15% of total sales will be cash sales and the rest will be on credit. The balance of trade receivables at 1 May 20X6 was £10,000 and the company expects trade receivables at the end of July 20X6 will be 60% of the credit sales for the quarter.

2 All purchases are to be made on credit terms. The balance of trade payables at 1 May 20X6 was £1,200. Total payments for purchases during the quarter will be £2,000.

3 Expenses include a depreciation charge of £250. All other expenses are settled on cash terms.

4 The carrying value of the non-current assets at 1 May 20X6 was £20,000 and the carrying value at 31 July 20X6 is forecast to be £24,000. The company will pay for any additions immediately by cash.

5 The tax payable shown in the statement of financial position was £2,600 at 1 May 20X6 and is expected to be £2,800 at 31 July 20X6

6 The cash position at 1 May 20X6 was £30,000.

**Calculate the closing cash position at 31 July 20X6. Use brackets or minus signs where appropriate.**

|  | £ |
| --- | --- |
| Operating profit |  |
| Change in inventory |  |
| Change in receivables |  |
| Change in payables |  |
| Adjustment for non-cash items |  |
| Purchase of non-current assets |  |
| Tax paid |  |
| Net change in cash position |  |
| Cash position 1 May 20X6 |  |
| Forecast cash position 31 July 20X6 |  |

12  The following forecast information has been provided for a business for the next year 20X6:

|  | £ | £ |
| --- | --- | --- |
| Revenue |  | 600,000 |
| Less:  Cost of sales |  |  |
| Opening inventory | 50,000 |  |
| Purchases | 200,000 |  |
| Closing inventory | (50,000) |  |
|  | ——— |  |
|  |  | (200,000) |
|  |  | ——— |
| Gross profit |  | 400,000 |
| Expenses |  | (150,000) |
|  |  | ——— |
| Operating profit |  | 250,000 |
| Tax |  | (52,500) |
|  |  | ——— |
| Profit after tax |  | 197,500 |

**Additional information**

1    The company believes that 90% of total sales will be credit sales and the rest will be cash. The balance of trade receivables at 1 January 20X6 was £100,000 and the company expects trade receivables at the end of December 20X6 to be 20% of the credit sales for the year.

2    All purchases are to be made on credit terms. The balance of trade payables at 1 January 20X6 was £50,000. Total payments for purchases during the year will be £230,000.

3    Expenses include a depreciation charge of £25,000. All other expenses are settled on cash terms.

4    The carrying value of the non-current assets at 1 January 20X6 was £20,000 and the carrying value at 31 December 20X6 is forecast to be £24,000. In March 20X6 the business will take out a new finance lease to acquire a new machine that would otherwise cost £15,000. The finance lease is repayable at £625 per month. The finance lease has not been included in the forecast financial statements.

5    The tax payable shown in the statement of financial position was £50,000 at 1 January 20X6 and is expected to be £55,000 at 31 December 20X6

6    The forecast cash position at 1 January 20X6 was £70,000 in hand

**Calculate the closing cash position at 31 December 20X6. Use brackets or minus signs where appropriate.**

|  | £ |
|---|---|
| Operating profit |  |
| Change in inventory |  |
| Change in receivables |  |
| Change in payables |  |
| Adjustment for non-cash items |  |
| Purchase of non-current assets |  |
| Tax paid |  |
| Net change in cash position |  |
| Cash position 1 January 20X6 |  |
| Forecast cash position 31 December 20X6 |  |

**13**    Style Limited is a clothing manufacturer. Extracts from the trial balance at 31 March 20X5 for Style Limited's were as follows:

|  | £000 | £000 |
|---|---|---|
| 6% loan notes (redeemable 20Y0) |  | 1,500 |
| Administrative expenses | 1,540 |  |
| Cash and cash equivalents | 822 |  |
| Cost of sales | 3,463 |  |
| Distribution costs | 1,590 |  |
| Inventory at 31 March 20X5 | 1,320 |  |
| Land and buildings at cost | 5,190 |  |
| Plant and equipment at cost | 3,400 |  |
| Accumulated depreciation at 31 March 20X4: Buildings |  | 1,500 |
| Accumulated depreciation at 31 March 20X4: Plant and equipment |  | 1,659 |
| Revenue |  | 8,210 |

**Additional information provided:**

(i)    There were no sales or purchases of non-current assets or available for sale investments during the year ended 31 March 20X5.

(ii)    Income tax due for the year ended 31 March 20X5 is estimated at £250,000. There is no balance outstanding in relation to previous years' corporate income tax. The deferred tax provision needs to be increased by £100,000.

(iii)    Depreciation is charged on buildings using the straight-line basis at 3% each year. The cost of land included in land and buildings is £2,000,000. Plant and equipment is depreciated using the reducing balance method at 20%. Depreciation is regarded as a cost of sales.

(iv)    Style Limited entered into a non-cancellable five year operating lease on 1 April 20X4 to acquire machinery to manufacture a new range of kitchen units. The cost of the operating lease is to be shared over the life of the lease in the statement of profit or loss. Under the terms of the lease, Style Limited will receive a payment holiday for the first year, then £62,500 is payable for four years commencing in year two of the lease. The machine is estimated to have a useful economic life of 20 years. The cost of the lease is regarded as a cost of sales.

(v)    The 6% loan notes are 10 year loans due for repayment March 20Y0. Style Limited incurred no other finance costs in the year to 31 March 20X5.

**Prepare the statement of profit or loss for Style Limited for the year to 31 March 20X5.**

**Style Limited's statement of profit or loss for the year ended 31 March 20X5**

|  | £000 |
|---|---|
| Revenue |  |
| Cost of sales |  |
|  | ——— |
| Gross profit |  |
| Administrative expenses |  |
| Distribution costs |  |
|  | ——— |
| Operating profit |  |
| Finance cost |  |
|  | ——— |
| Profit before tax |  |
| Income tax expense |  |
|  | ——— |
| Profit for the period |  |

**14** The accounting books of Ruby and Daughters are incomplete, however it was possible to find out the following information.

The 20X5 accounts showed the following closing balances:

| | |
|---|---|
| Non-current assets | £50,000 |
| Inventory | £5,000 |
| Receivables | £12,000 |
| Cash at bank | £33,000 |
| Cash in hand | £2,000 |
| Payables | £7,000 |

The cash account at the end of 20X6 showed the following:

**Cash account**

| | £ | | £ |
|---|---|---|---|
| Balance b/d | 2,000 | Bankings | 38,000 |
| Cash from customers | 40,000 | Wages | 800 |
| | | Sundry expenses | 200 |
| | | Balance c/d | 3,000 |
| | 42,000 | | 42,000 |

The bank account at the end of 20X6 showed the following:

**Bank account**

| | £ | | £ |
|---|---|---|---|
| Balance b/d | 33,000 | Salaries | 20,000 |
| Bankings from cash | 38,000 | Rent | 5,000 |
| | | Credit purchases | 25,000 |
| | | Drawings | 10,000 |
| | | Balance c/d | 11,000 |
| | 71,000 | | 71,000 |

A review of outstanding sales invoices, unpaid at the year-end showed a total of £16,000.

Ruby says that the business currently owes about £5,000 for building materials.

Inventory levels have increased by 20% from the start of the year.

At year-end there is a sundry expense accrual of £50 and a rent prepayment of £300.

Depreciation is to be provided at 20% on carrying value.

**Prepare a statement of profit or loss for the year 20X6.**

**Ruby and Daughters**

**Statement of profit or loss for the year**

|  | £ | £ |
|---|---|---|
| Sales | | |
| Opening inventory | | |
| Purchases | | |
| Less: Closing inventory | | |
| | ——— | |
| Cost of sales | | |
| | | ——— |
| Gross profit | | |
| Less: | | |
| Wages and salaries | | |
| Rent | | |
| Sundry expenses | | |
| Depreciation | | |
| | ——— | |
| | | ——— |
| Net profit/(loss) | | |
| | | ——— |

15    The following extracts from the financial statements are available:

| Extracts from the budget statement of financial position | Period 3 £000 | Period 4 £000 | Extracts from the budgeted income statement | Period 3 £000 | Period 4 £000 |
|---|---|---|---|---|---|
| NBV Non-current assets | 930 | 858 | Turnover | 720 | 760 |
| Trade receivables | 445 | 423 | Purchases | (718) | (427) |
| Car lease payments | 6 | 5 | Other expenses | (110) | (126) |
| Cash | 13 | 15 | Car leasing | (12) | (13) |
| Trade payables | (435) | (433) | Depreciation | (65) | (60) |
| | | | Loss on disposal of a non-current asset | – | (3) |

Additional information

1    Cash sales represent 10% of turnover

2    The receipt from the disposal of the non-current asset occurs in the same period the disposal is made.

Using the information above, complete the period 4 extract of the cash budget. Use minus signs where appropriate.

| Extract of the cash budget | Period 4 £000 |
|---|---|
| Receipts of cash sales | |
| Receipts from trade receivables | |
| Receipt from disposal of non-current asset | |
| Car lease payments | |

# FORECASTING

## MOVING AVERAGES

16  A company is preparing its forecast sales and purchase information for January.

The sales volume trend is to be identified using a 3–point moving average based on the actual monthly sales volume.

(a)  Complete the table below to calculate the current monthly sales volume trend and identify any monthly variations using the additive model.

| | Sales volume (units) | Trend | Monthly variation |
|---|---|---|---|
| May | 61,600 | | |
| June | 39,100 | | |
| July | 55,300 | | |
| August | 72,100 | | |
| September | 49,600 | | |
| October | 65,800 | | |
| November | 82,600 | | |
| December | 60,100 | | |

**Additional information**

The selling price per unit has been set at £14.50.

Monthly purchases are estimated to be 30% of the value of the forecast sales.

(b)  Using the trend and the monthly variations identified in part (a) complete the table below to forecast the sales volume, sales value and purchase value for January of the next financial year.

| | Forecast trend | Variation | Forecast sales volume | Forecast sales £ | Forecast purchases £ |
|---|---|---|---|---|---|
| January | | | | | |

**17** A company is preparing its forecast sales and purchase information for December.

The sales volume trend is to be identified using a 5–point moving average based on the actual monthly sales volumes.

(a) **Complete the table below to calculate the current monthly sales volume trend and identify any monthly variations using the additive model.**

| | Sales volume (units) | Trend | Monthly variation |
|---|---|---|---|
| January | 19,906 | | |
| February | 22,390 | | |
| March | 20,555 | | |
| April | 18,666 | | |
| May | 21,333 | | |
| June | 20,156 | | |
| July | 22,640 | | |
| August | 20,805 | | |
| September | 18,916 | | |
| October | 21,583 | | |
| November | 20,406 | | |

**Additional information**

The selling price per unit has been set at £30.

Monthly purchases are estimated to be 28% of the value of the forecast sales.

(b) **Using the trend and the monthly variations identified in part (a) calculate the forecast purchases value for December.**

| | Forecast purchases £ |
|---|---|
| December | |

**18** A company is preparing its forecast sales and purchase information.

The sales volume trend is to be identified using a 3–point moving average based on the actual monthly sales volumes.

(a) **Complete the table below to calculate the current monthly sales volume trend and identify any monthly variations using the multiplicative model.**

| | Sales volume (units) | Trend | Monthly variation (2 dp) |
|---|---|---|---|
| October | 6,408 | | |
| November | 8,816 | | |
| December | 9,686 | | |
| January | 6,934 | | |
| February | 9,520 | | |
| March | 10,440 | | |
| April | 7,460 | | |
| May | 10,225 | | |

(b) **The average monthly trend (to the nearest whole number) is** [        ]

**19** **(a)** **Which of the following are illustrations of a seasonal variation? (Tick two)**

| | |
|---|---|
| Sales of footballs increase when the world cup is on. | |
| Sales of greetings cards increase in December. | |
| Sales of milk remain constant all year. | |
| Sales of houses increase in Spring. | |
| Sales of newspapers rise whenever it rains. | |

**(b)** **Which of the following is an illustration of a cyclical variation? (Tick one)**

| | |
|---|---|
| Tennis rackets sales increase during Wimbledon. | |
| Over summer, more hosepipes are sold. | |
| Sales of raincoats increase in April. | |
| During the last general election, sales of ice-cream increased. | |
| Sales of diet books reach a peak after every Olympics. | |

**(c)** **Complete the sentences below by picking the correct options.**

A seasonal variation is a change in sales which occurs **[at regular intervals, normally of less than a year/at random/regularly but not every year]** whereas a cyclical variation occurs **[at the same time every year/at random/over a long time period]**.

The underlying sales trend is the sales level excluding **[seasonal variation/random variation/cyclical variation/all variations]**.

**20** **(a)** **Which of the following are illustrations of a seasonal variation? (Tick two)**

| | |
|---|---|
| Sales of houses increase when the England cricket team wins. | |
| Sales of wrapping paper increase in November and December. | |
| Sales of venetian blinds have been falling consistently for 3 years. | |
| Sales of wallpaper increase at the same time that sales of toothpaste fall. | |
| Sales of shoes rise in summer. | |

**(b)** **Which of the following is an illustration of a cyclical variation? (Tick one)**

| | |
|---|---|
| Tennis rackets sales decrease when it rains. | |
| Over summer, more ice creams are sold. | |
| Sales of gloves increase in Autumn. | |
| When Sky HD was launched a carpet firm in Cardiff experienced 20% sales growth. | |
| Over the last 50 years the average price of oil has increased for 5 years, then decreased for 5 years. This pattern continued over the 50 year period. | |

## MARK-UP AND MARGIN

**21** If purchases are £900 (assuming purchases are the only component of the cost of sales)

 (a) **What would sales be if a 40% mark-up was applied?**

 (b) **What would the sales be if the sales margin was 40%?**

**22** A company is preparing its forecast sales and purchase information for October.

The sales volume trend is to be identified using a 3–point moving average based on the actual monthly sales volumes.

 (a) **Complete the table below to calculate the current monthly sales volume trend and identify any monthly variations using the additive model.**

| | Sales volume (units) | Trend | Monthly variation |
|---|---|---|---|
| February | 10,100 | | |
| March | 10,950 | | |
| April | 11,650 | | |
| May | 11,000 | | |
| June | 11,850 | | |
| July | 12,550 | | |
| August | 11,900 | | |
| September | 12,750 | | |

The monthly variation in July is [          ] units.

 **Additional information**

The selling price per unit has been set at £21.50.

 (b) **Using the trend and the monthly variations identified in part (a) complete the table below to forecast the sales volume and sales value for October.**

| | Forecast trend | Variation | Forecast sales volume | Forecast sales £ |
|---|---|---|---|---|
| October | | | | |

 (c) **If the company has a margin of 20%, assuming that purchases are the only component of the cost of sales, the value of the purchases will be £ _____.**

 (d) **If the company adds a mark-up of 25%, assuming that purchases are the only component of the cost of sales, the value of the purchases will be £ _____.**

**23** Jacob Limited is a manufacturing company, specialising in a single product, the 'Benji'. The company's yearend is 31 December.

The company is organised in two divisions: Manufacturing and Sales.

When goods are completed they are transferred from Manufacturing to Sales at full production cost plus a 5% mark up.

The Sales division is then responsible for onward sale to external customers. The Sales department applies a 10% mark up to calculate the selling price.

A few sales to external customers (with a 7% margin applied) are made by the Manufacturing division directly (i.e. without going through Sales).

The table below contains the total purchase costs of the units sold in the first 3 months of 20X0.

| | Manufacturing Division | | |
| --- | --- | --- | --- |
| | *To external customers* | *To Sales Division* | *Total* |
| | £ | £ | £ |
| *20X0* | | | |
| January | 51 | 230 | 281 |
| February | 60 | 140 | 200 |
| March | 18 | 132 | 150 |

**Calculate the value of the total monthly sales value to external customers for the first 3 months of 20X0 (round to the nearest penny).**

## INDEXING

**24** The price of biscuits is set on the first day of every month. The price for the last four months is given below.

**Create an index for the price of biscuits using month 3 as the base period.**

| Month | 1 | 2 | 3 | 4 | 5 | 6 | 7 |
| --- | --- | --- | --- | --- | --- | --- | --- |
| Price | 0.12 | 0.15 | 0.21 | 0.32 | 0.26 | 0.25 | 0.30 |
| Index | | | | | | | |

**25** The company uses an industry wage rate index to forecast future monthly wage costs. Employees receive a pay increase in October each year. The monthly wage cost of £20,500 was calculated when the wage index was 131.

The forecast wage rate index for the next three months is:

August        142
September     146
October       151

**If the company uses the forecast wage rate index, what will the wage cost for October be, to the nearest £?**

A      £30,955

B      £20,651

C      £23,630

D      £22,899

**26**    Four years ago material X cost £5 per kg and the price index most appropriate to the cost of material X stood at 150. The same index now stands at 430.

**What is the best estimate of the current cost of material X per kg?**

A    £1.74

B    £9.33

C    £14.33

D    £21.50

**27**    Two years ago the price index appropriate to the cost of material Y had a value of 120. It now has a value of 160.

**If material Y costs £2,000 per kg today, what would the cost per kg have been two years ago?**

A    £1,500

B    £1,667

C    £2,667

D    £3,200

**28**    **(a)**    **Using the following information calculate the missing figures for the sales price (to 2 decimal places) and index, using the information for Period 1 as a base.**

| Period | 1 | 2 | 3 | 4 | 5 |
|---|---|---|---|---|---|
| Sales price £ | 40.00 | 55.00 | | 48.00 | |
| Index | 80.00 | | 120.00 | | 121.00 |

**(b)**    **If the company was making a margin of 20% on the sales price, what was the cost price in period 1?**

£

29 A company has its own temperature-regulated greenhouses to enable year round growing of herbs and other ingredients. They are preparing the forecast purchases of manure (in tonnes) for next year. The sales volume trend is to be identified using a 3-month moving average.

(a) **Complete the table below, calculate the monthly purchases volume trend and identify any monthly variations. Enter minus signs where appropriate, and round to the nearest whole number.**

| Month | Purchases volume (tonnes) | Trend | Monthly variation |
|-------|---------------------------|-------|-------------------|
| 1 | 5,150 | | |
| 2 | 5,241 | | |
| 3 | 5,487 | | |
| 4 | 5,615 | | |
| 5 | 5,280 | | |
| 6 | 5,456 | | |
| 7 | 5,648 | | |
| 8 | 5,890 | | |
| 9 | 5,448 | | |
| 10 | 5,689 | | |
| 11 | 5,847 | | |
| 12 | 6,000 | | |

(b) **Calculate the average monthly trend to the nearest whole number.**

(c) **Calculate the forecast purchases trend for month 17 and 18.**

| Month 17 (tonnes) | Month 18 (tonnes) |
|-------------------|-------------------|
| | |

The purchase price per tonne in month 7 was £56 when the cost index was 125. The cost index for month 18 is expected to be 142.

(d) **Calculate the purchase cost for month 18**

## REGRESSION ANALYSIS

**30** The overhead costs of RP have been found to be represented by the formula:

$$y = £10,000 + £0.25x$$

where y is the monthly cost and x represents the activity level measured as the number of orders.

Monthly activity levels of orders may be estimated using a combined regression analysis and time series model:

$$a = 100,000 + 30b$$

where a represents the de-seasonalised monthly activity level and b represents the month number.

In month 240, the seasonal index value is 108.

**Calculate the overhead cost for RP for month 240 to the nearest £1,000.**

**31** Z plc has found that it can estimate future sales using time series analysis and regression techniques. The following trend equation has been derived:

$$y = 25,000 + 6,500x$$

where

y is the total sales units per quarter

x is the time period reference number

Z has also derived the following set of seasonal variation index values for each quarter using a multiplicative model:

| | |
|---|---|
| Quarter 1 | 70 |
| Quarter 2 | 90 |
| Quarter 3 | 150 |
| Quarter 4 | 90 |

**Using the above model, calculate the forecast for sales units for the third quarter of year 7, assuming that the first quarter of year 1 is time period reference number 1.**

**The following data relate to Questions 32 and 33.**

H is forecasting its sales for next year using a combination of time series and regression analysis models. An analysis of past sales units has produced the following equation for the quarterly sales trend:

$$y = 26x + 8,850$$

where the value of x represents the quarterly accounting period and the value of y represents the quarterly sales trend in units. Quarter 1 of next year will have a value for x of 25.

The quarterly seasonal variations have been measured using the multiplicative (proportional) model and are:

Quarter 1      − 15%
Quarter 2      − 5%
Quarter 3      + 5%
Quarter 4      + 15%

Production is planned to occur at a constant rate throughout the year.

The company does not hold inventories at the end of any year.

**32**   **The difference between the budgeted sales for quarter 1 and quarter 4 next year are:**

   A      78 units

   B      2,850 units

   C      2,862 units

   D      2,940 units

**33**   **The number of units to be produced in each quarter of next year will be nearest to:**

   A      9,454 units

   B      9,493 units

   C      9,532 units

   D      9,543 units

**34** A company is preparing its annual budget and is estimating the number of units of Product A that it will sell in each quarter of Year 2. Past experience has shown that the trend for sales of the product is represented by the following relationship:

y = a + bx where

y = number of sales units in the quarter

a = 10,000 units

b = 3,000 units

x = the quarter number where 1 = quarter 1 of Year 1

Actual sales of Product A in Year 1 were affected by seasonal variations and were as follows:

Quarter 1:          14,000 units

Quarter 2:          18,000 units

Quarter 3:          18,000 units

Quarter 4:          20,000 units

**Calculate the expected sales of Product A (in units) for each quarter of Year 2, after adjusting for seasonal variations using the additive model.**

**35** Production overhead costs at company BW are assumed to vary with the number of machine hours worked. A line of best fit will be calculated from the following historical data, with costs adjusted to allow for cost inflation over time.

| Year | Total production Overheads £ | Number of machine hours | Cost index |
|------|------------------------------|-------------------------|------------|
| 20X8 | 143,040 | 3,000 | 192 |
| 20X9 | 156,000 | 3,200 | 200 |
| 20Y0 | 152,320 | 2,700 | 224 |
| 20Y1 | 172,000 | 3,000 | 235 |

**(a)    Restate the cost data at the 20Y1 price level, to remove differences caused by inflation.**

If the line of best fit, based on current (20Y1) prices, is calculated as:

y = 33,000 + 47x

where y = total overhead costs in £ and x = machine hours:

**(b)    Calculate the expected total overhead costs in 20Y2 if expected production activity is 3,100 machine hours and the expected cost index is 250.**

**36    CFV**

If a forecasting model based on total cost = fixed cost + variable costs is graphed, the equation is C = F + Vx and the intercept is £7,788.

**If total costs are £14,520 and × is 3,300 then the gradient of the line, to two decimal places, is _____.**

# PATTERNS OF CASH FLOW

## CASH RECEIPTS

**37** An enterprise commenced business on 1 April 20X2. Revenue in April 20X2 was £20,000, and this is expected to increase at 2% a month. Cash sales represent the other 40% of revenue. Of the remaining sales the cash receipts are predicted to be 30% one month after sale, 65% two months after sale. The balance is potential irrecoverable debts, a provision is charged in the month of sale

(i) **Calculate how much cash is expected to be received in June 20X2**

(ii) **Calculate the forecast closing receivables balance at the end of June 20X2**

(iii) **Calculate the irrecoverable debt provision for May 20X2**

**38** Jane limited sold 5,000 units of its only product in July 20X5 at a selling price of £60 each. Due to an increase in production costs, this price increases to £65 with effect from 1 August 20X3 and this is expected to reduce demand for August to 4,000 units. Thereafter, however, demand is expected to increase by 10% per month.

Cash sales account for 2,500 units per month and are expected to remain at this level. Credit sales account for the balance and receivables pay as follows:

(a) 60% by value in the month of sale, receiving a 2% discount

(b) 40% by value in the following month.

Credit sales in June were £103,500

**What are the budgeted cash receipts in July, August and September 20X5?**

**39** Levison Entertainment has been trading for a number of years. Levison's owner, Phil, has called and asked for help in calculating their cash and credit sales. Actual sales values achieved are available for January and February and forecast sales values have been produced for March to June.

| | Actual | | Forecast | | | |
|---|---|---|---|---|---|---|
| | January | February | March | April | May | June |
| Total sales £ | 61,000 | 72,000 | 54,000 | 72,500 | 81,600 | 92,000 |

Levison Entertainment estimates that cash sales account for 8% of the total sales. The remaining 92% of sales are made on a credit basis. Levison Entertainment estimates that 30% of credit sales are received in the month after sale with the balance being received two months after sale.

(a) **Calculate the timing of the credit sales receipts that would be included in a cash budget for Levison Entertainment for the period March to June.**

| | March | April | May | June |
|---|---|---|---|---|
| Monthly credit sales receipts £ | | | | |

(b) **The trade receivables balance at the end of June is forecast to be £ _____.**

**40**   Razor Bodyboards estimates that cash sales account for 15% of the total sales. The remaining 85% of sales are made on a credit basis.

| | January | February | March |
|---|---|---|---|
| Total sales | 51,000 | 62,000 | 44,000 |

Razor estimates that 60% of credit sales are received in the month after sale with 40% being received two months after sale.

**(a)   The receipts from both cash and credit sales to be shown in the cash budget for March will be?**

A   £48,960

B   £50,120

C   £55,560

D   £58,260

**(b)   The trade receivables balance at the end of March is forecast to be £ _____ .**

**41**   M Jones has been trading for a number of years. Sales volume has been forecast for January to May. Each picture sells for 20p.

Martin estimates that cash sales account for 40% of the total sales. The remaining sales are made on a credit basis.

Martin estimates that 60% of credit sales are received in the month after sale with the balance being received two months after sale.

| | January | February | March | April | May |
|---|---|---|---|---|---|
| Sales volume (pictures) | 1,500 | 2,000 | 1,800 | 1,900 | 2,100 |

**Complete the table below to identify the total sales receipts forecast for April and May.**

| | April | May |
|---|---|---|
| Total sales receipts £ | | |

**Calculate the trade receivables balance at the end of May.**

The trade receivables balance at the end of May is forecast to be £_____

**42**   Canvas Canopies has been trading for a number of years. The business has supplied information regarding its forecast sales, purchases and expenses.

Sales values have been forecast for January to May.

Canvas Canopies estimates that cash sales account for 15% of the total sales. The remaining 85% of sales are made on a credit basis.

| | January | February | March | April | May |
|---|---|---|---|---|---|
| Total sales £ | 8,000 | 10,000 | 15,000 | 18,000 | 23,000 |

Canvas Canopies estimates that 70% of credit sales are received in the month after sale with the balance being received two months after sale.

(a) **Complete the table below to calculate the total sales receipts forecast for April and May.**

|  | April £ | May £ |
|---|---|---|
| Total sales receipts |  |  |

(b) **Identify the forecast trade receivables balance at the end of May.**

The trade receivables balance at the end of May is forecast to be:

£_____

43 The sales information for the second 3 months of 20X2 for 'Light my Fire' is as follows:

- Sales to the retail trade are expected to be 120,000 candles in April, 125,000 in May and 130,000 in June. In addition we expect to sell 5,000 candles from our own shop in each of the next three months.

- Candles will be sold to the retail trade at £1.65. Sales made from our own shop will be made at £3 each.

- Sales from our own shop will be made for cash.

- Although it is our policy for all trade customers to pay within 30 days, for budgetary purposes you should assume that 30% of retail trade customers pay one month after the date of sale and 70% pay two months after the date of sale.

- The credit sales in February 20X2 were £145,000 and March 20X2 were £150,000.

**Complete the table below to show the cash inflows for April to June 20X2**

|  | April | May | June |
|---|---|---|---|
| Cash sales |  |  |  |
| Credit sales receipts |  |  |  |
| Total receipts |  |  |  |

44 Shirley Ltd has been trading for a number of years. Shirley's owner, Kelly, has called and asked for help in calculating their cash and credit sales.

The company receives cash for 50% of its sales. The balance of its revenue is received 30 days after sales.

Estimated sales figures and prices for the four months to 31st December 20Y1 are as follows:

|  |  | September | October | November | December |
|---|---|---|---|---|---|
| Sales units | 000s | 20 | 15 | 17 | 18 |
| Selling price per unit | £ | 30 | 40 | 40 | 50 |

**Calculate the cash inflows for October to December 20Y1.**

|  | October | November | December |
|---|---|---|---|
| Cash sales |  |  |  |
| Credit sales receipts |  |  |  |
| Total cash received |  |  |  |

**45** Surfers Paradise Enterprises has been trading for a number of years.

Actual figures are available for April and May and forecast figures have been produced for June to September.

Cash sales account for 25% of the total sales. The remaining 75% of sales are made on a credit basis.

|  | Actual | | Forecast | | | |
|---|---|---|---|---|---|---|
|  | April | May | June | July | August | September |
| Total sales £ | 12,500 | 16,000 | 13,353 | 15,153 | 14,400 | 16,660 |

Surfers Paradise Enterprises estimates that 40% of credit sales are received in the month after sale, 20% two months after sale, with the balance being received three months after sale.

**Calculate the credit sales receipts ready to include in a cash budget for Surfers Paradise Enterprises.**

|  | July £ | August £ | September £ |
|---|---|---|---|
| Credit sales receipts |  |  |  |

**46** A company has the following budgeted sales figures:

| Month 1 | £90,000 |
|---|---|
| Month 2 | £105,000 |
| Month 3 | £120,000 |
| Month 4 | £108,000 |

80% of sales are on credit and the remainder are paid in cash. Credit customers paying in the month after sale are given a discount of 1.5%. Credit customers normally pay within the following time frame:

1 month after sale     40% of credit sales

2 months after sale     70% of credit sales

3 months after sale     98% of credit sales

There is an expectation that 2% of credit sales will become irrecoverable debts.

**Calculate the total receipts expected in month 4.**

## CASH PAYMENTS

47 A company has a budget, for two products A and B, as follows:

|  | Product A | Product B |
|---|---|---|
| Sales (units) | 2,000 | 4,500 |
| Production (units) | 1,750 | 5,000 |
| Labour: |  |  |
| Skilled at £10/hour | 2 hours/unit | 2 hours/unit |
| Unskilled at £7/hour | 3 hours/unit | 4 hours/unit |

**Calculate the total labour cost to be included in the budget.**

48 A job requires 2,400 standard labour hours for completion but it is anticipated that idle time will be 20% of the total time budgeted. If the wage rate is £10 per hour, what is the budgeted labour cost for the job, including the cost of the idle time?

A £19,200

B £24,000

C £28,800

D £30,000

49 M Jones pays his suppliers on the basis of 20% one month after date of purchase, 50% two months after purchase and the remainder three months after the date of purchase.

At the end March the balance on the trade payables is forecast to be:

|  | £ |
|---|---|
| January | 570 |
| February | 2,000 |
| March | 2,500 |
| Trade payables at the end of March | 5,070 |

**Complete the table below to identify the value of trade payable at the end of March that will be paid in April and May.**

|  | April £ | May £ |
|---|---|---|
| Settlement of trade payable |  |  |

50 Tarleton Ltd is preparing cash payment figures for a new division ready for inclusion in a cash budget. The following information is relevant to purchases of raw material.

|  | July £ | August £ | September £ | October £ | November £ | December £ |
|---|---|---|---|---|---|---|
| Opening inventory | 4,000 | 8,400 | 9,100 | 9,000 | 11,600 | 12,600 |
| Purchases | 5,500 | 5,750 | 6,000 | 6,250 | 6,500 | 6,750 |
| Closing inventory | (8,400) | (9,100) | (9,000) | (11,600) | (12,600) | (13,500) |
| Cost of sales | 1,100 | 5,050 | 6,100 | 3,650 | 5,500 | 5,850 |

The company pays its supplier on the basis of 40% one month after the date of purchase and 60% two months after purchase.

(a)    **At the end of September the balance of the trade payables is forecast to be:**

£ _____

(b)    **Complete the table below to identify the value of trade payables that will be paid in October and November.**

|  | October £ | November £ |
|---|---|---|
| Purchases |  |  |

51    Canvas Canopies pays their suppliers on the basis of 40% one month after date of purchase, 20% two months after purchase and the remainder three months after the date of purchase.

At the end May the balance on the trade payables is forecast to be:

|  | £ |
|---|---|
| January | 5,280 |
| February | 8,640 |
| March | 16,800 |
| Trade payables at the end of March | 30,720 |

(a)    **Complete the table below to identify the value of trade payables at the end of March that will be paid in April and May.**

|  | April £ | May £ |
|---|---|---|
| Settlement of trade payables |  |  |

A new machine is to be purchased in January at a total cost of £60,000. Payment for the machine is to be made in three equal monthly instalments, beginning in January.

The machine is to be depreciated monthly on a straight-line basis at 20% per annum. This has been included in the expenses of the business.

Expenses are paid in the month they are incurred.

(b)    **Complete the table below to show the expenses to be included in the cash budget.**

|  | January £ | February £ | March £ | April £ | May £ |
|---|---|---|---|---|---|
| Expenses | 4,512 | 4,951 | 5,541 | 5,745 | 6,785 |
| Total cost to be included in cash budget |  |  |  |  |  |

**52** North Ltd is preparing cash payment figures ready for inclusion in a cash budget. The following information is relevant to the payment patterns for purchases, wages and expenses.

- Monthly production is based on the following month's sales figure.

- Estimated sales for the four months to 31st December 20Y1 are as follows:

| | | September | October | November | December |
|---|---|---|---|---|---|
| Sales units | 000s | 20 | 15 | 15 | 15 |

- The sales volume figure for January 20Y2 is estimated to be 40,000 units.

- All trade payable amounts relate to raw materials. Raw materials are purchased in the month they are required and are paid for after 30 days. The raw material cost per unit is £8.

- Direct Labour is paid at the rate of £7 per hour and each unit takes 2 hours to make.

- North's Administration costs amount to a fixed amount of £90,000 per month. However, this includes a £30,000 depreciation cost.

- Production costs amount to £10 per unit which is paid in the month that it is incurred – this figure includes a £3 per unit depreciation cost.

- Distribution costs are calculated as 10% of the direct labour cost and are paid in the month incurred.

- A new machine is to be purchased and installed in the factory in October 20Y1. The company will have to pay the 1st part of the purchase fee of £300,000 in September, followed by a further £300,000 in October. A final payment of £25,000 is to be made one month later.

**Prepare an extract of the payments section of the cash budget for North Ltd for the three months ended December.**

| | October £000 | November £000 | December £000 |
|---|---|---|---|
| Trade payables | | | |
| Direct labour | | | |
| Administration cost | | | |
| Production costs | | | |
| Distribution costs | | | |
| Non-current asset purchase | | | |
| **Total payments** | | | |

**53** South Ltd is preparing cash payment figures for inclusion in a cash budget. The following information is relevant to the payment patterns for purchases, wages and expenses.

- Purchases are calculated as 42% of the next month's forecast sales and are paid two months after the date of purchase.

|  | Actual | | | Forecast | | |
|---|---|---|---|---|---|---|
|  | Jan £ | Feb £ | Mar £ | Apr £ | May £ | June £ |
| Total sales | 100,000 | 120,000 | 118,000 | 124,000 | 130,000 | 136,000 |

- Wages are paid in the month that they are incurred and expenses are paid the month after they are incurred. The actual and forecast figures for wages and expenses are:

|  | Actual | | | Forecast | | |
|---|---|---|---|---|---|---|
|  | Jan £ | Feb £ | Mar £ | Apr £ | May £ | June £ |
| Wages | 7,000 | 7,200 | 7,250 | 7,800 | 8,100 | 8,500 |
| Expenses | 11,000 | 11,100 | 12,000 | 12,200 | 12,400 | 12,900 |

- A new machine is to be purchased in February at a total cost of £39,000. Payment for the machine is to be made in three equal monthly instalments, beginning in March.

**What is the total cash out flow in May?**

A   £82,860

B   £85,380

C   £85,580

D   £87,900

**54** Bailey Rae Ltd produces garden gnomes.

Labour costs include hourly paid employees and four-weekly paid employees. The labour costs for hourly paid employees are calculated based on the number of hours worked multiplied by a standard hourly rate of £12. Hourly paid employees are paid overtime at a premium of 25%. The company also employs a supervisor who receives an annual salary of £23,400. The year is divided into 13 four week periods.

Any overtime payments are paid in the following period, once the overtime has been signed off.

|  | February £ | March £ | April £ | May £ |
|---|---|---|---|---|
| Forecast standard hours | 2,000 | 1,800 | 1,950 | 1,850 |
| Forecast overtime hours | 200 | 150 | 170 | 120 |

**Calculate the total payments for labour in April and May.**

|  | April | May |
|---|---|---|
| Total labour costs |  |  |

**55** Jump Ltd purchases raw materials from Bounce Ltd for £15 per unit. Purchases were 19,000 units for period 7 and 20,500 units for period 8. Forecast purchases for the rest of the year are as follows:

| Units | Period 9 | Period 10 | Period 11 | Period 12 |
|---|---|---|---|---|
| Purchases | 20,000 | 21,000 | 20,500 | 22,000 |

Jump Ltd currently pays Bounce Ltd as follows:

- Period of purchase 10%

- Period following period of purchase 50%

- Balance to be paid two periods following the period of purchase

A competitor to Bounce Ltd has started offering the same raw materials at a price of £10 per unit and would be able to start supplying to Jump Ltd in Period 9. However their payment terms are:

- Period of purchase 60%

- Period following the period of purchase 40%

Bounce Ltd has realised that their competitor is undercutting their prices, and is now offering Jump Ltd the following settlement discounts and payment terms for period 9 and onwards

**Option 1** 12% discount for making full payment in the period of purchase

**Option 2** 6% discount for making a payment of 50% in the period of purchase and the remaining 50% in the period following the period of purchase

**Calculate the forecast cash payments in periods 10, 11 and 12 under the current purchase and payments terms, if Jump Ltd changed supplier and for each of the two discount options from Bounce Ltd.**

| | Period 10 £ | Period 11 £ | Period 12 £ |
|---|---|---|---|
| Current terms | | | |
| Competitor terms | | | |
| Option 1 | | | |
| Option 2 | | | |

**56** D plc operates a retail business. Purchases are sold at cost plus 25%. The management team is preparing the cash budget and has gathered the following data:

1   The budgeted sales are as follows:

| Month | £000 |
|---|---|
| July | 100 |
| August | 90 |
| September | 125 |
| October | 140 |

2   It is management policy to hold inventory at the end of each month which is sufficient to meet sales demand in the next half month. Sales are budgeted to occur evenly during each month.

3   Payables are paid one month after the purchase has been made.

Calculate the entries for 'purchases' that will be shown in the cash budget for:

(i)     August

(ii)    September

(iii)   October

**57**     A business pays its suppliers on the basis of 20% one month after the date of purchase, 50% two months after the date of purchase and 30% three months after the date of purchase.

At the end of June the balance of trade payables is forecast to be:

|  | £ |
|---|---|
| Balance from April | 6,000 |
| Balance from May | 19,200 |
| Balance from June | 28,400 |
| Trade payables at the end of June | 53,600 |

**Complete the table to identify the value of trade payables at the end of June that will be collected in July and August**

|  | July £ | August £ |
|---|---|---|
| Settlement of trade payables |  |  |

**58**     The direct labour costs for a business include both standard working hours and overtime. These costs are split between 80% standard working hours and 20% overtime.

Standard working hours are paid in the month worked whilst overtime is paid in the following month. In addition to this; a performance bonus is paid quarterly; the next payment will be in September and will be £125,000. The overtime for June was £90,000.

In addition to the direct labour costs, employer's National Insurance payments are 10% for standard working hours and 12% for overtime and the performance bonus. This is paid in the month following payment of the appropriate element of the direct labour cost. The outstanding payment for the June employer's National Insurance is £ 32,000.

The direct labour costs are as follows:

July £340,000

August £360,000

September £350,000

October £400,000

**(a)**     Calculate the total payments made in July, August, September and October for direct labour costs, performance bonus and employer's National Insurance contributions.

| Month | July | August | September | October |
|---|---|---|---|---|
| Total payment |  |  |  |  |

**(b)**     What are the employer's National Insurance contributions on the overtime paid in November?

## CASH BUDGETS

**59** The following data are available for GHK Ltd for June, July and August:

|  | June £ | July £ | August £ |
|---|---|---|---|
| Sales | 45,000 | 50,000 | 60,000 |
| Wages | 12,000 | 13,000 | 14,500 |
| Overheads | 8,500 | 9,500 | 9,000 |

The following information is available regarding direct materials:

|  | June £ | July £ | August £ | September £ |
|---|---|---|---|---|
| Opening inventory | 5,000 | 3,500 | 6,000 | 4,000 |
| Material usage | 8,000 | 9,000 | 10,000 |  |
| Closing inventory | 3,500 | 6,000 | 4,000 |  |

**Notes:**

1  10% of sales are for cash, the balance is received the following month. The amount to be received in June for May's sales is £29,500.

2  Wages are paid in the month they are incurred.

3  Overheads include £1,500 per month for depreciation. Overheads are settled the month following. £6,500 is to be paid in June for May's overheads.

4  Direct materials are paid for in the month purchased.

5  The opening cash balance in June is £11,750.

6  A tax bill of £25,000 is to be paid in July.

**Required:**

**(a)  Calculate the amount of direct material purchases in EACH of the months of June, July and August.**

**(b)  Prepare cash budgets for June, July and August.**

**(c)  Describe briefly the benefits of preparing cash budgets.**

**60** Campbell Ltd buys goods in bulk from a French manufacturing company, packs them and then sells them on to retailers.

- Sales for May and June 20X6 were £10,000 each month and are forecast to increase by 10% each month from July 20X6 onwards.

- There are no cash sales and receivables are expected to settle as follows:

  (i)  25% in the month of sale

  (ii)  60% in the month following sale

  (iii)  15% in month two months after sale.

- Loose product (unpacked) is bought in the month in which it is sold. Purchases for May and June were €7,080 each month, and are forecast to increase by 9% each month from July onwards. Suppliers allow one month's credit. The exchange rate is €1:£0.7203

- Packaging costs amount to £1,800 per month paid in the month incurred.

- Sundry expenses amount to £800 per month.

- Depreciation is £1,000 per month.

- At 30 June 20X6, the bank balance was £6,000 overdrawn.

**Prepare a cash flow forecast for the 3 months ended 30 September 20X6 (round your values to the nearest whole pound).**

61 The cash budget for SDS Ltd for the three months ended August has been partially completed. The following information is to be incorporated and the cash budget completed.

- A bank loan of £30,000 has been negotiated and this will be paid into the business bank account in July.

- The loan term is 10 months beginning in August. Interest of 8% is added at the beginning of the loan term and monthly repayments include both capital and interest elements.

- New fixtures and fittings are to be purchased in July at a cost of £10,000. The cost is to be spread over 5 monthly instalments starting in August.

- If SDS uses its bank overdraft facility, interest is payable monthly and is estimated at 2% of the previous months overdraft balance. The interest is to be rounded to the nearest £.

- At 1 June the balance of the bank overdraft was £5,000.

**Using the information above, complete the cash budget for SDS for the three months ending August.**

Cash inflows should be entered as positive figures and cash outflows as negative figures. Zeroes must be entered where appropriate to achieve full marks.

|  | June £ | July £ | August £ |
|---|---|---|---|
| **RECEIPTS** |  |  |  |
| Cash sales | 1,100 | 1,200 | 2,300 |
| Credit sales | 40,810 | 60,540 | 70,990 |
| Bank loan |  |  |  |
| **Total receipts** |  |  |  |
| **PAYMENTS** |  |  |  |
| Purchases | −42,111 | −20,804 | −41,305 |
| Wages | −18,000 | −11,000 | −12,100 |
| Expenses | −2,555 | −1,543 | −1,100 |
| Capital expenditure |  |  |  |
| Bank loan repayment |  |  |  |
| Overdraft interest |  |  |  |
| **Total payments** |  |  |  |
| **Net cash flow** |  |  |  |
| Opening bank balance |  |  |  |
| Closing bank balance |  |  |  |

**62**   The cash budget for Bank Industries for the three months ended 30th June needs to be completed using the following information.

- Actual and forecast sales are as follows:

|  | Actual | | Forecast | | |
| --- | --- | --- | --- | --- | --- |
|  | February | March | April | May | June |
| Total sales £ | 32,500 | 34,800 | 40,500 | 42,000 | 45,750 |

- 20% of cash is received in the month of sale, 30% one month after sale and the remainder two months after sale.

- Credit purchases were £15,000 in February and are forecast to increase by 4% each month. Payments are made one month after purchase.

- Wages are forecast to be £8,000 each month.

- Other expenses, paid one month in arrears, are as follows:

|  | Actual | | Forecast | | |
| --- | --- | --- | --- | --- | --- |
|  | February | March | April | May | June |
| Expenses  £ | 5,000 | 4,750 | 4,950 | 5,125 | 5,050 |

- A bank loan of £100,000 has been negotiated and this will be paid into the business bank account in April. The loan term is 20 months beginning in May. Interest is to be paid at £50 per month for the first year, starting in May.

- When Bank Industries uses its bank overdraft facility, interest is payable monthly and is estimated at 2% of the previous month's overdraft balance. The interest is to be rounded to the nearest £.

- Bank Industries has to pay tax of £60,000 in April.

- At 1 April the balance of the bank account was £50,000 in credit.

**Using the information above, complete the cash budget for Bank Industries for the three months ending June.**

Cash inflows should be entered as positive figures and cash outflows as negative figures. Zeroes must be entered where appropriate to achieve full marks. Round your answers to the nearest whole £.

|  | April £ | May £ | June £ |
|---|---|---|---|
| **RECEIPTS** | | | |
| Cash sales | | | |
| Credit sales | | | |
| Bank loan | | | |
| **Total receipts** | | | |
| **PAYMENTS** | | | |
| Purchases | | | |
| Wages | | | |
| Expenses | | | |
| Tax payment | | | |
| Bank loan repayment | | | |
| Overdraft interest | | | |
| **Total payments** | | | |
| **Net cash flow** | | | |
| Opening bank balance | | | |
| Closing bank balance | | | |

63 The cash budget for Surfers Paradise Enterprises for the three months ended 30 September needs to be completed.

- Actual and forecast sales are as follows:

|  | Actual | | Forecast | | |
|---|---|---|---|---|---|
|  | May | June | July | August | September |
| Total sales £ | 9,000 | 10,500 | 11,000 | 13,000 | 16,000 |

- 15% of cash is received in the month of sale, 45% one month after sale and the remainder two months after sale.

- Credit purchases were £7,000 in June and are forecast to increase by 3% each month. Payments are made one month after purchase.

- Wages are forecast to be £4,000 each month.

- Other expenses, paid one month after being incurred, are as follows:

|  | Actual | | Forecast | | |
|---|---|---|---|---|---|
|  | May | June | July | August | September |
| Expenses £ | 1,500 | 1,250 | 1,750 | 2,000 | 1,800 |

- A bank loan of £12,960 has been negotiated and this will be paid into the business bank account in July. The loan attracts 10% interest calculated on the amount of the loan advanced in July. The interest is added at the beginning of the loan term. The capital and interest elements of the bank loan are to be repaid in 36 equal monthly instalments beginning in August.

- Surfers Paradise Enterprises receives 0.5% interest based on a credit closing balance, received one month in arrears. The interest is to be rounded to the nearest £.

- Overdraft interest is payable monthly and is estimated at 1% of the previous month's overdraft balance. The interest is to be rounded to the nearest £.

- Surfers Paradise Enterprises will be making a dividend payment to shareholders of £15,000 in July.

- At 1 July the balance of the bank account was £3,600 in credit.

**Using the information above, complete the cash budget for Surfers Paradise Enterprises for the three months ending 30th September.**

Cash inflows should be entered as positive figures and cash outflows as negative figures. Zeroes must be entered where appropriate to achieve full marks. Round your answers to the nearest whole £.

|  | July £ | August £ | September £ |
|---|---|---|---|
| **RECEIPTS** | | | |
| Cash sales | | | |
| Credit sales | | | |
| Bank loan | | | |
| Interest receivable | | | |
| **Total receipts** | | | |
| **PAYMENTS** | | | |
| Purchases | | | |
| Wages | | | |
| Expenses | | | |
| Dividend payment | | | |
| Bank loan repayment | | | |
| Overdraft interest | | | |
| **Total payments** | | | |
| **Net cash flow** | | | |
| Opening bank balance | | | |
| Closing bank balance | | | |

**64** Jump Ltd has provided the following partially completed cash budget for month 3 and month 4. Further information has been provided to determine the cash inflows and outflows from the company.

- The company rents out part of its property with effect from month 4. The rent is £31,200 per annum and is payable in equal monthly instalments on the first day of each month.

- The company has got £500,000 invested in a fixed rate account, paying interest of 5% per annum. The company has chosen to have this interest paid monthly.

- The company received payment for the sale of a non-current asset in month 3. The profit from the sale was £7,000 and the asset originally cost £48,000 and has been depreciated by 50%. (Ignore VAT)

- The company bought a non-current asset in month 2. The new asset cost £54,000 and paid 45% in month 2. The remaining balance is to be paid in six equal instalments commencing in month 3. (Ignore VAT).

- The company has a mortgage on their premises. The purchase cost of the premises was £750,000 and the mortgage is 80% LTV. The mortgage is for 15 years and interest is charged on the initial balance at 4.5% per annum. Payments are made monthly.

- Jump Ltd prepares its VAT return for the previous quarter ending month 12. The sales for the quarter were £510,100 net with purchases of £340,100. The VAT rate is 20%. Any VAT payment or refund with be made or received in month 3.

- The bank balance for Month 3 was £160,000

**Using the information provided, complete the cash balance for the company for Month 3 and 4.**

**Note**

- Cash inflows should be entered as positive figures

- Cash outflows should be entered as negative figures (use brackets or minus sign)

- Round to the nearest whole pound throughout

- If a cell does not require an entry, leave it blank

|  | Month 3 £ | Month 4 £ |
|---|---|---|
| **RECEIPTS** | | |
| Sales receipts | 672,450 | 682,670 |
| Rental income | | |
| Investment income | | |
| Sale of non-current asset | | |
| **Total receipts** | | |
| **PAYMENTS** | | |
| Purchases | –40,150 | –50,200 |
| Wages and salaries | –94,700 | –92,100 |
| General Expenses | –6,000 | –5,000 |
| Mortgage payment | | |
| VAT payment to HMRC | | |
| Purchase of non-current assets | | |
| Overdraft interest | | |
| **Total payments** | | |
| **Net cash flow** | | |
| Opening bank balance | | |
| Closing bank balance | | |

65 The cash budget for Gibbon Ltd has been partially completed for two periods. The following information is to be incorporated and the cash budget completed.

- In an earlier period Gibbon Ltd made an insurance claim of £125,000. The insurer rejected 10% of this claim and will make a payment to Gibbon Ltd of 80% of the accepted liability in period 4, the remainder will be made in period 6

- The US subsidiary is due to pay a dividend of USD 50,000 in period 5. The exchange rate to be used to convert the receipt into GBP is USD 1.22:GBP 1

- A statue was purchased in period 3. It cost £10,000 and will be sold with a margin of 20% in period 5.

- Following the retirement of the CEO, a recruitment company was employed to search for a replacement. This person has been found and appointed. The fees and commission amount to a flat rate of £7,000 plus 20% of the starting salary of £150,000, payable in Period 5.

- Payroll cost for period 4 to 6 are in the table below. 12% of the payroll represents normal deductions from employees which are paid to HMRC in the month following the month that the cost is incurred. The employees receive their pay on the last Thursday of the month in which their pay is earned. The employer's NIC is paid to HMRC at the same time the employees' deductions are paid.

| Forecast data | Period 4 | Period 5 | Period 6 |
|---|---|---|---|
| Payroll | 80,000 | 80,300 | 80,500 |
| Employer's NIC | 16,000 | 16,060 | 16,100 |

**Using the information, complete the cash budget for the company for periods 5 and 6**

**Note:**

- Cash inflows should be entered as positive figures

- Cash outflows should be entered as negative figures (use brackets)

- Round to the nearest whole pound throughout

- If a cell does not require an entry, leave it blank

| Cash budget | Period 5 £ | Period 6 £ |
|---|---|---|
| Receipts | | |
| Receipts from sales | 100,500 | 106,250 |
| Insurance claim | | |
| Dividend receipt | | |
| Receipt from sale of statue | | |
| Total receipts | | |
| Payments | | |
| Purchases | (8,510) | (9,400) |
| Payroll payments to employees | | |
| Payments to HMRC | | |
| Recruitment cost of the CEO | | |
| Other expenses | (12,050) | (16,507) |
| Total payments | | |
| Net cash flow | | |
| Opening bank balance | 8,250 | |
| Closing bank balance | | |

# SENSITIVITY ANALYSIS

**66  Complete the following sentences by selecting the correct options:**

Offering prompt payment discounts to customers should **[increase/decrease]** the time taken to recover debts. However, it will also **[increase/reduce]** the total cash received.

**67  Complete the following sentence by selecting the correct options:**

Taking advantage of early settlement discounts offered by suppliers will **[increase/reduce]** the amount we pay overall but having to pay **[earlier/later]** may mean there is a **[bigger/smaller]** strain on our cash flows.

**68** A cash budget has been prepared for Worsley Ltd for the next five periods.

The budget was prepared based on the following sales volumes and a selling price of £50 per item.

|  | Period 1 | Period 2 | Period 3 | Period 4 | Period 5 |
|---|---|---|---|---|---|
| Sales volume (items) | 1,800 | 1,900 | 2,050 | 1,890 | 2,150 |

The pattern of cash receipts used in the budget assumed 30% of sales were received in the month of sale and the remaining 70% in the month following sale.

In the light of current economic trends, Worsley Ltd needs to adjust its cash budget to take account of the following:

- The selling price from period 1 will be reduced by 20% per item.

- The pattern of sales receipts changes to 10% of sales received in the month of sale, 50% in the month following sale and the remaining 40% two months after sale.

(a) **Use the table below to calculate the effect of the changes in the forecast amounts and timing of cash receipts for periods 3, 4 and 5:**

|  | Period 1 £ | Period 2 £ | Period 3 £ | Period 4 £ | Period 5 £ |
|---|---|---|---|---|---|
| Original value of forecast sales |  |  |  |  |  |
| Original timing of receipts |  |  |  |  |  |
| Revised value of forecast sales |  |  |  |  |  |
| Revised timing of receipts |  |  |  |  |  |

The company has managed to negotiate extended payment terms with its suppliers. The original budget was prepared on the basis of paying suppliers in the month following purchase. The revised payment terms allow for settlement of 20% in the month following purchase with the remaining payment two months after purchase.

The original budgeted purchases figures were:

|  | Period 1 £ | Period 2 £ | Period 3 £ | Period 4 £ | Period 5 £ |
|---|---|---|---|---|---|
| Purchases | 21,200 | 22,354 | 28,601 | 21,660 | 29,500 |

(b) **Use the table below to calculate the effect of the changes in the timing of purchase payments for periods 3, 4 and 5:**

|  | Period 3 £ | Period 4 £ | Period 5 £ |
|---|---|---|---|
| Original timing of payments |  |  |  |
| Revised timing of payments |  |  |  |

Worsley Ltd has always tried to operate without utilising a bank overdraft and the original cash budget identified that an overdraft would not be required for periods 3, 4 or 5.

(c)  Using your calculations from parts (a) and (b), complete the table to show the effect of the changes to sales receipts and purchase payments on the budgeted bank balance for periods 3, 4 and 5.

|  | Period 3 £ | Period 4 £ | Period 5 £ |
|---|---|---|---|
| Original net cash flow | 5,632 | 5,162 | 5,893 |
| Changes in sales receipts |  |  |  |
| Changes in purchase payments |  |  |  |
| Revised net cash flow |  |  |  |
| Opening bank balance | 8,597 |  |  |
| Closing bank balance |  |  |  |

69  A cash budget has been prepared for Jones Ltd for the next five periods.

The budget was prepared based on the following sales volumes and a selling price of £150 per item.

|  | Period 1 | Period 2 | Period 3 | Period 4 | Period 5 |
|---|---|---|---|---|---|
| Sales volume (items) | 800 | 900 | 650 | 890 | 750 |

The pattern of cash receipts used in the budget assumed 20% of sales were received in the month of sale and the remaining 80% in the month following sale.

In the light of current economic trends, Jones Ltd needs to adjust its cash budget to take account of the following:

- The sales volume for each period will be reduced by 30%.

- The pattern of sales receipts changes to 20% of sales received in the month of sale, 60% in the month following sale and the remaining 20% two months after sale.

(a)  Use the table below to calculate the effect of the changes in the forecast amounts and timing of cash receipts for periods 3, 4 and 5:

|  | Period 1 £ | Period 2 £ | Period 3 £ | Period 4 £ | Period 5 £ |
|---|---|---|---|---|---|
| Original value of forecast sales |  |  |  |  |  |
| Original timing of receipts |  |  |  |  |  |
| Revised value of forecast sales |  |  |  |  |  |
| Revised timing of receipts |  |  |  |  |  |

Purchases are based on the budgeted sales volume for the next month. Each item is purchased for £90. Jones Ltd has managed to negotiate extended payment terms with its suppliers. The original budget was prepared on the basis of paying suppliers in the month following purchase. The revised payment terms allow for settlement of 60% in the month following purchase with the remaining payment two months after purchase.

**(b)** **Use the table below to calculate the effect of the changes in the timing of purchase payments for periods 3, 4 and 5:**

| | Period 3 £ | Period 4 £ | Period 5 £ |
|---|---|---|---|
| Original timing of payments | | | |
| Revised timing of payments | | | |

Jones Ltd has always tried to operate without utilising a bank overdraft and the original cash budget identified that an overdraft would not be required for periods 3, 4 or 5.

**(c)** **Using your calculations from parts (a) and (b), complete the table to show the effect of the changes to sales receipts and purchase payments on the budgeted bank balance for periods 3, 4 and 5.**

| | Period 3 £ | Period 4 £ | Period 5 £ |
|---|---|---|---|
| Original net cash flow | 52,362 | 51,986 | 53,695 |
| Changes in sales receipts | | | |
| Changes in purchase payments | | | |
| Revised net cash flow | | | |
| Opening bank balance | 18,597 | | |
| Closing bank balance | | | |

**70** A cash budget has been prepared for a new division of TanTan Ltd for the next five periods.

The budget was prepared based on the following sales volumes and a selling price of £95 per item.

| | Period 1 | Period 2 | Period 3 | Period 4 | Period 5 |
|---|---|---|---|---|---|
| Forecast sales £ | 95,000 | 104,500 | 99,750 | 152,000 | 166,250 |

The pattern of cash receipts used in the budget assumed 30% of sales were received in the month of sale and the remaining 70% in the month following sale.

| | Period 1 | Period 2 | Period 3 | Period 4 | Period 5 |
|---|---|---|---|---|---|
| Original forecast sales receipts £ | 28,500 | 97,850 | 103,075 | 115,425 | 156,275 |

TanTan Ltd wishes to encourage payment of debts so it is going to introduce a settlement discount for early repayment. The pattern of sales receipts is planned to be:

- 60% of sales received in the month of sale with a discount of 2%
- 30% in the month following sale
- 10% two months after sale.

**(a)** **Complete the table below to calculate the sales receipts expected in periods 1–5:**

|  | Period 1 £ | Period 2 £ | Period 3 £ | Period 4 £ | Period 5 £ |
|---|---|---|---|---|---|
| Period 1 sales |  |  |  |  |  |
| Period 2 sales |  |  |  |  |  |
| Period 3 sales |  |  |  |  |  |
| Period 4 sales |  |  |  |  |  |
| Period 5 sales |  |  |  |  |  |
| Revised forecast sales receipts |  |  |  |  |  |

**(b)** **Complete the sentence below:**

Total receipts from sales in periods 1 to 3 **increase/decrease** by _____% if the settlement discount is offered.

**71** A cash budget has been prepared for Higson Ltd for the next five periods.

The budget was prepared based on the following sales volumes and a selling price of £18 per item.

|  | Period 1 | Period 2 | Period 3 | Period 4 | Period 5 |
|---|---|---|---|---|---|
| Sales volume (items) | 1,800 | 1,900 | 2,050 | 1,890 | 2,150 |

The pattern of cash receipts used in the budget assumed 35% of sales were received in the month of sale, 25% in the month following sale and 40% two months after sale.

Higson Ltd has heard that one of its customers is going out of business and will not be ordering any more goods from them. This customer had planned to buy 500 units in period 1 and 250 units in period 3. The budget needs to be adjusted to take account of this.

**(a)** **Use the table below to calculate the effect of the changes in the forecast amounts of the cash receipts for periods 3, 4 and 5:**

|  | Period 1 £ | Period 2 £ | Period 3 £ | Period 4 £ | Period 5 £ |
|---|---|---|---|---|---|
| Original value of forecast sales | 32,400 | 34,200 | 36,900 | 34,020 | 38,700 |
| Revised value of forecast sales |  |  |  |  |  |
| Original timing of receipts |  |  | 34,425 | 34,812 | 36,810 |
| Revised timing of receipts |  |  |  |  |  |

Purchases are based on the budgeted sales volume for the next month. The company will be able to adjust the purchases based on the changes in sales. Each item costs £10 to buy. The budget was prepared on the basis of paying suppliers 35% in the month following purchase with the remaining payment two months after purchase.

**(b)** **Use the table below to calculate the effect on the cash flow of the changes in the volume of purchases for periods 3, 4 and 5:**

|  | Period 3 £ | Period 4 £ | Period 5 £ |
|---|---|---|---|
| Payment for purchases |  |  |  |

Higson Ltd has always tried to operate without utilising a bank overdraft, and the original cash budget identified that an overdraft would not be required for periods 3, 4 or 5.

**(c)** **Calculate from the budgeted bank balance at the end of period 5.**

|  | £ |
|---|---|
| Opening bank balance period 3 | 3,200 |
| Total sales receipts |  |
| Total purchase payments |  |
| Closing bank balance period 5 |  |

**72** A cash budget has been prepared for Barossa Ltd for the next five periods.

The budget was prepared based a selling price of £14 per item.

|  | Period 1 | Period 2 | Period 3 | Period 4 | Period 5 |
|---|---|---|---|---|---|
| Sales value £ | 30,100 | 30,800 | 32,620 | 31,640 | 33,600 |

The pattern of cash receipts used in the budget assumed 50% of sales were received in the month of sale and the remaining 50% in the month following sale.

In the light of current economic trends, Barossa Ltd needs to adjust its cash budget to take account of the following:

- The selling price from period 1 will be reduced by 5% per item.
- The sales volume will also be reduced by 8% (round to the nearest whole item).
- The pattern of sales receipts changes to 15% of sales received in the month of sale, 40% in the month following sale and the remaining 45% two months after sale.

**(a)** **Use the table below to calculate the revised forecast sales and revised timing of cash receipts for periods 3, 4 and 5:**

|  | Period 1 £ | Period 2 £ | Period 3 £ | Period 4 £ | Period 5 £ |
|---|---|---|---|---|---|
| Revised value of forecast sales |  |  |  |  |  |
| Revised timing of receipts |  |  |  |  |  |

The company has managed to negotiate new payment terms with its suppliers. The original budget was prepared on the basis of paying suppliers in the month following purchase. The revised payment terms allow for settlement of 40% in the month of purchase with a 3% settlement discount, 30% in the month following purchase with the remaining payment two months after purchase.

The original budgeted purchase figures were:

|  | Period 1 £ | Period 2 £ | Period 3 £ | Period 4 £ | Period 5 £ |
|---|---|---|---|---|---|
| Purchases | 8,580 | 7,600 | 6,820 | 10,740 | 11,310 |

(b) **Use the table below to calculate the revised timing of purchase payments for periods 3, 4 and 5:**

|  | Period 3 £ | Period 4 £ | Period 5 £ |
|---|---|---|---|
| Revised timing of payments |  |  |  |

Barossa Ltd has always tried to operate without utilising a bank overdraft and the original cash budget identified that an overdraft would not be required for periods 3, 4 or 5.

(c) **Using your calculations from parts (a) and (b) plus the information regarding the original receipts and payments, complete the table to show the effect of the changes to sales receipts and purchase payments on the budgeted bank balance for periods 3, 4 and 5.**

|  | Period 3 £ | Period 4 £ | Period 5 £ |
|---|---|---|---|
| Original net cash flow | 276 | 153 | 219 |
| Changes in sales receipts |  |  |  |
| Changes in purchase payments |  |  |  |
| Revised net cash flow |  |  |  |
| Opening bank balance | 790 |  |  |
| Closing bank balance |  |  |  |

73 The draft cash budget of Splish Inc shows the following:

|  | Period 1 £ | Period 2 £ | Period 3 £ |
|---|---|---|---|
| Receipts | 70,000 | 75,000 | 78,000 |
|  |  |  |  |
| Payments |  |  |  |
| Purchases | 15,000 | 17,500 | 18,900 |
| Other production expenses | 6,000 | 6,200 | 6,700 |
| Wages and salaries | 8,250 | 8,800 | 9,000 |
| Rent | 12,000 | 12,000 | 12,000 |
| Total Payments | 41,250 | 44,400 | 46,500 |

**Additional information** has now been received:

- A trade discount of 4% has been negotiated on purchases, with no change in payment pattern
- Other production expenses will increase by 7%, with no change in payment pattern
- Wages and salaries are paid in the month they are incurred, and a pay rise of 2.5% has been agreed which will come into effect in period 2
- Rent is paid one month in advance and rent will increase by £400 in period 3.

**(a)** Prepare a revised payments schedule to take account of the changes outlined above. Do not use minus figures.

|  | Period 1 £ | Period 2 £ | Period 3 £ |
|---|---|---|---|
| Payments | | | |
| Purchases | | | |
| Other production expenses | | | |
| Wages and salaries | | | |
| Rent | | | |
| Total payments | | | |

**(b)** The effect of the changes to payments is to **increase/decrease** the quarterly cash outflows by £_____.

**74** The draft cash receipts and payments budget for a company for the quarter to March has been prepared as follows:

|  | January £ | February £ | March £ | Total £ |
|---|---|---|---|---|
| Sales receipts | 30,000 | 24,000 | 35,000 | 89,000 |
| Payments | | | | |
| Material | 7,500 | 6,000 | 8,750 | 22,250 |
| Labour | 9,000 | 7,200 | 10,500 | 26,700 |
| Overheads | 7,500 | 6,600 | 8,250 | 22,350 |

- When the budget was set the selling price was £20. It has been decided to increase the selling price by 10% but this will reduce volume by 12%. All sales are made on a cash basis.

- Material cost is £5 per unit made. Materials are paid for in the month of purchase and no inventory of material is maintained.

- Each unit is forecast to take 0.5 hours to make. Labour is paid at £12 per hour. Due to the learning effect it is now taking employees 0.25 hours to make a unit and, to reward this new efficiency, wages have been increased to £14 per hour.

- Overheads include a fixed cost of £3,000 and a variable cost of £3 per unit.

**(a)** Prepare revised figures for the cash budget for January to March.

|  | January £ | February £ | March £ | Total £ |
|---|---|---|---|---|
| Sales receipts | | | | |
| Payments | | | | |
| Material | | | | |
| Labour | | | | |
| Overheads | | | | |

The opening cash balance for January was £14,750.

(b) **Calculate the original cash balance at the end of March and then calculate the revised cash balance once the budgeted amendments have been applied. Use minus signs to indicate a negative impact on the cash balance.**

| | £ |
|---|---|
| Original closing cash balance at 31 March | |
| Change in sales receipts | |
| Change in material cost | |
| Change in labour cost | |
| Change in overhead cost | |
| Revised closing cash balance at 31 March | |

**Calculate the effect the above will have on the cash flow of the company for periods 1 to 3.**

The cumulative cash flow for period 1 to 3 will **increase/decrease** by £ ☐

75  Yanu plc is planning on replacing some of its machinery. It will cost £1.5 million and will be paid in equal amounts in periods 1 and 2. The new machines will increase productivity by 10,000 units a period; all these units will be sold in the month of production at £50 each. The cash will be received 50% in the month of sale and 50% the month following sale.

**Calculate the effect the above will have on the cash flow of the company for periods 1 to 3.**

The cumulative cash flow for period 1 to 3 will **increase/decrease** by £ ☐

76  Kovich Ltd thinks that they will need to pay overtime due to increased production for the next 4 weeks. The overtime premium is 50% of the normal hourly wage. The total overtime payment is £10.50. It is thought that the hours will increase by 25%, currently there are 50 employees, working a 37 hour week. The extra production will lead to an increase in units available to sell. The increase in sales will amount to an extra £25,000 in cash receipts.

**Calculate the effect the above will have on the cash flow of Kovich Ltd over the next 4 weeks.**

The cumulative cash flow for the next four weeks will **increase/decrease** by £ ☐

77  Gibbons Ltd has an agreement to pay its major supplier for purchases as follows:

30% in month of purchases

25% in the month following purchase

45% two months following month of purchase

**The value of the materials expected to be purchased in January, February, March and April is as follows:**

January £230,000

February £290,000

March £230,000

April £270,000

The supplier has announced that a discount of 2% will be offered on all purchases over £250,000 if payment is received in the month of sale. To take advantage of this Gibbon Ltd has decided to equally divide its expected purchases over the next four months but will pay as follows:

50% in the month of purchase

10% in the month following the month of purchase

40% two months following month of purchase

As January is the start of the new reporting period, Gibbon Ltd has decided to pay all outstanding trade payables at the end of December.

(a) **Calculate the forecast purchase payments in January, February, March and April, taking advantage of the discount on the revised payment terms. VAT can be ignored.**

| Month | January £ | February £ | March £ | April £ |
|---|---|---|---|---|
| Forecast purchase payments | | | | |

(b) **Calculate the total savings made over the four months on the revised payment terms.**

## MONITORING CASH BUDGETS

78  The quarterly budget and actual figures for Heavier Goth Ltd are provided below:

| | Budget £ | Actual £ |
|---|---|---|
| Receipts from receivables | 65,664 | 58,844 |
| Cash sales | 2,890 | 3,844 |
| Payments to payables | (46,666) | (35,100) |
| Cash purchases | (1,000) | (1,200) |
| Capital expenditure | – | (24,500) |
| Wages and salaries | (7,690) | (5,600) |
| General expenses | (17,500) | (16,000) |
| Net cash flow | (4,302) | (19,712) |
| Opening bank balance | 7,500 | 7,500 |
| Closing bank balance | 3,198 | (12,212) |

(a) **Prepare a reconciliation of budgeted cash flow with actual cash flow for the quarter. Select the appropriate description for each entry.**

|  | Variance £ | Adverse/Favourable |
|---|---|---|
| Budgeted closing bank balance |  |  |
| Receipts from receivables |  |  |
| Cash sales |  |  |
| Payments to payables |  |  |
| Cash purchases |  |  |
| Capital expenditure |  |  |
| Wages and salaries |  |  |
| General expenses |  |  |
| Actual closing bank balance |  |  |

(b) **What action could the organisation have taken to avoid an overdrawn bank balance (select one option)?**

A    Chased customers to pay sooner and delayed payments to payables

B    Increased cash sales through better marketing

C    Delayed capital expenditure

D    Negotiated lower wages payments to employees

(c) **Match each cause of a variance listed on the left with a possible course of action on the right.**

| | |
|---|---|
| Rates of income tax have increased labour costs | Improve credit control |
| Customers are buying lower value products | Change suppliers |
| Suppliers are insisting on earlier payments | Reduce hours worked |
| Customers are taking more days to settle their debts | Negotiate early settlement discount |
| Prices of raw materials have increased | Actively market more expensive product lines |

**79** The budget and actual figures for GFD Ltd are provided below, along with the variances.

|  | Budget £ | Actual £ | Variance £ |
|---|---|---|---|
| Receipts from receivables | 9,664 | 8,844 | 820 A |
| Cash sales | 890 | 844 | 46 A |
| Payments to payables | (3,666) | (5,100) | 1,434 A |
| Cash purchases | (100) | (1,200) | 1,100 A |
| Capital expenditure | – | (14,500) | 14,500 A |
| Wages and salaries | (690) | (600) | 90 F |
|  |  |  |  |
| Net cash flow | 6,098 | (11,712) |  |
| Opening bank balance | 500 | 500 |  |
|  |  |  |  |
| Closing bank balance | 6,598 | (11,212) |  |

(a) **Provide possible reasons why the variances might have occurred.**

(b) **Suggest corrective actions and identify implications for future budget setting, where appropriate.**

**80** **Complete the table below by calculating the missing figures.**

Use minus signs (not brackets) where appropriate and put A into the table to denote an adverse difference and F to denote a favourable difference.

|  | Budgeted £ | Actual £ | Variance £ | A/F |
|---|---|---|---|---|
| RECEIPTS |  |  |  |  |
| Cash sales | 4,200 | 3,800 |  |  |
| Credit sales |  | 48,000 | 5,900 | F |
| Total receipts |  |  |  |  |
|  |  |  |  |  |
| PAYMENTS |  |  |  |  |
| Cash purchases | −500 |  | 700 | A |
| Credit purchases |  | −35,100 | 7,100 | A |
| Labour costs | −2,500 | −3,200 |  |  |
| Capital expenditure | −8,000 | −6,000 |  |  |
| General expenses | −4,000 |  | 200 | F |
| Total payments |  |  |  |  |
|  |  |  |  |  |
| Net cash flow |  |  |  |  |

**81** The quarterly budget and actual figures for an organisation are provided below:

| | Budget £ | Actual £ |
|---|---|---|
| Receipts from receivables | 56,423 | 51,667 |
| Cash sales | 7,350 | 6,780 |
| Payments to payables | (42,618) | (44,791) |
| Cash purchases | (5,600) | (6,540) |
| Capital expenditure | – | (12,000) |
| Wages and salaries | (6,200) | (2,600) |
| General expenses | (6,600) | (2,464) |
| | | |
| Net cash flow | 2,755 | (9,948) |
| Opening bank balance | 3,700 | 3,700 |
| | | |
| Closing bank balance | 6,455 | (6,248) |
| | | |

(a) **Prepare a reconciliation of budgeted cash flow with actual cash flow for the quarter.**

| | £ | Adverse or favourable |
|---|---|---|
| Budgeted closing bank balance | | |
| Receipts from receivables | | |
| Cash sales | | |
| Payments to payables | | |
| Cash purchases | | |
| Capital expenditure | | |
| Wages and salaries | | |
| General expenses | | |
| Actual closing bank balance | | |

(b) **Explain what actions the organisation should have taken to avoid an overdrawn bank balance?**

82    The budget and actual figures for SPR Ltd are provided below. A variance which is 5% or more of the original budget is deemed to be significant and needs to be investigated.

|  | Budgeted £ | Actual £ |
|---|---|---|
| RECEIPTS |  |  |
| Credit sales | 95,651 | 89,891 |
| Investment income | 15,360 | 12,569 |
| Total receipts | 111,011 | 102,460 |
|  |  |  |
| PAYMENTS |  |  |
| Cash purchases | 8,354 | 8,369 |
| Credit purchases | 47,532 | 48,985 |
| Labour costs | 2,200 | 2,000 |
| Capital expenditure | 25,000 | 32,000 |
| General expenses | 5,951 | 5,713 |
| Total payments | 89,037 | 97,067 |
|  |  |  |
| Net cash flow | 21,974 | 5,393 |

Further information has been made available:

•    A machine in the production department broke down and had to be replaced.

•    There has been a recent reduction in the bank base rate from 1.5% to 0.5%

**Identify each of the significant variances for the period. Provide possible reasons why the variance might have occurred, suggest corrective actions where appropriate, and identify implications for future budget setting.**

# LIQUIDITY MANAGEMENT

## WORKING CAPITAL CYCLE/CASH OPERATING CYCLE

83    **Which one of the following is the main function of liquidity management?**

A    keeping cash in the bank

B    making a profit

C    meeting any liabilities due

D    investing in capital expenditure

84    **Which one of the following is the liquid asset?**

A    Land

B    Trade receivables

C    Inventory

D    Savings account

**85**  A business has an average inventory holding period of 80 days, receives payment from its customers in 40 days and pays its payables in 45 days.

**What is the cash operating cycle, in days, for the business?**

A       120 days

B       165 days

C       75 days

D       5 days

**86**  **If a business increases its inventory holding period by 5 days and increases the time it takes to pay its payables by 7 days, what is the impact on the cash operating cycle?**

**87**  **If a business increases its receivable collection period by 10 days and decreases its inventory holding period by 3 days, what is the impact on the cash operating cycle?**

**88**  AP had a balance outstanding on trade receivables at 30 September 20X6 of £68,000. Forecast credit sales for the next six months are £250,000 and customers are expected to return goods with a sales value of £2,500.

Based on past experience, within the next six months AP expects to collect £252,100 cash and to write off, as irrecoverable debts, 5% of the balance outstanding at 30 September 20X6.

**Calculate AP's forecast trade receivables days outstanding at 31 March 20X7.**

**89**  KAI's trade receivables balance at 1 April 20X6 was £22,000. KAI's statement of profit or loss showed revenue from credit sales of £290,510 during the year ended 31 March 20X7.

KAI's trade receivables at 31 March 20X7 were 49 days.

Assume KAI's sales occur evenly throughout the year and that all balances outstanding at 1 April 20X6 have been received.

Also, it should be assumed all sales are on credit, there were no irrecoverable debts and no trade discount was given.

**How much cash did KAI receive from its customers during the year to 31 March 20X7?**

A       £268,510

B       £273,510

C       £312,510

D       £351,510

**90**  A company has annual sales of £4 million, annual cost of sales of £3 million and makes annual purchases of £1.5 million. Its statement of financial position includes among assets and liabilities the following:

Trade receivables       £400,000

Trade payables          £300,000

Inventory               £800,000

**What is its cash operating cycle?**

**91** DX has gathered the following information for the year ended 31 May 20X5.

|  | 31 May 20X5 |
|---|---|
| Gross profit | 1,000,000 |
| Trade receivables | 290,000 |
| Trade payables | 190,000 |
| Trade receivables collection period in days | 44.1 |
| Inventory holding period in days | 93.9 |

(a) **Complete the table below (round your answers to the nearest 10,000 where appropriate).**

|  | 31 May 20X5 |
|---|---|
| Sales revenue |  |
| Cost of sales |  |
| Inventories level in the statement of financial position |  |
| Trade payables payment period in days |  |

(b) **The cash operating cycle for DX is** [　　　] **days**

**92** An extract from a company's trial balance at the end of its financial year is given below:

|  | £000 |
|---|---|
| Sales revenue (85% on credit) | 2,000 |
| Cost of sales | 1,800 |
| Purchases (90% on credit) | 1,650 |
| Inventory of finished goods | 220 |
| Trade receivables | 350 |
| Trade payables | 260 |

**Calculate the following working capital ratios:**

(i) Inventory days

(ii) Trade receivables days

(iii) Trade payables days

**93** The following figures have been extracted from the financial statements of a company for the year ended December 20X3.

| Statement of Financial Position (Extract) | £000 | Statement of Profit or Loss (Extract) | £000 |
|---|---|---|---|
| Inventories | 150 | Revenue | 2,700 |
| Receivables | 300 | Cost of sales | 1,300 |
| Cash | 25 | Gross profit | 1,400 |
| Payables | 230 | Admin costs | 500 |
| Overdraft | 90 | Distribution costs | 350 |
| | | Profit from operations | 550 |
| | | Finance cost | 75 |

(a) **Calculate the following (to the nearest day):**

The inventory holding period is_____days

The trade receivables collection period is _____days

The trade payables payment period is _____days

(b) **Using your answers to part (b) calculate the cash operating cycle for the company.**

The cash operating cycle is _____ days

**94** BDQ's annual sales are £100m of which 95% are made on credit. Receivables at the beginning of the year were £10 million and at the end of the year they were £12 million. 10% of receivables were non-trade related.

**What is BDQ's average collection period?**

A    36.5 days

B    40 days

C    38 days

D    46 days

**95** **Complete the following sentences by selecting the correct options:**

To improve the working capital cycle, a business could **[increase/decrease]** its debt collection period and/or **[extend/shorten]** the credit period it obtains from its suppliers.

**96** In October, a company made credit purchases of £18,000 and credit sales of £24,000. All sales are made on the basis of cost plus 25%.

**By how much will working capital increase in October as a result of these transactions?**

**97** A company has annual sales revenues of £30 million and the following working capital periods:

| | |
|---|---|
| Inventory conversion period | 2.5 months |
| Accounts receivable collection period | 2.0 months |
| Accounts payable payment period | 1.5 months |

Production costs represent 70% of sales revenue.

**Calculate the total amount held in working capital excluding cash and cash equivalents.**

**98** **Select the correct options to complete the following sentences:**

Over-capitalisation is a situation where a firm has **[more/less]** working capital than it needs.

**99** HL has been trading profitably, but has recently been accused of overtrading.

(i) **Explain the consequences of overtrading, and explain what is likely to happen if HL is overtrading.**

(ii) **Identify actions that HL could take to correct the problems of overtrading.**

## GOVERNMENT MONETARY POLICY AND REGULATIONS

**100** **What is the main reason why governments would not normally consider using quantitative easing to boost economic growth?**

A It would result in the government having to increase taxes to pay for it.

B It would generate high inflationary pressure.

C It would result in excessive savings, thus creating a leakage in the economy.

D It would crowd out private investment

**101** **Complete this sentence:**

Central banks try to increase the amount of lending and activity in the economy indirectly, by **lowering/raising** interest rates. **Lower/higher** interest rates encourage people to spend, not save.

**102** **What are the two main policies that Governments use to control the supply of money, interest rates and the availability of credit?**

(i)

(ii)

**103   What is the role of the treasury department in a trading company?**

(i)     Invest surplus funds

(ii)    Raise finance

(iii)   Reduce the tax liability

(iv)    To speculate on risky investments

A     (i) only

B     (i) and (ii) only

C     (i), (ii) and (iii)

D     All of the above

**104   Which one of the following is the Bank of England responsible for?**

A     Setting the APR for banks

B     Setting short term interest rates

C     Setting the corporation tax rate

D     Setting the VAT rate

**105   Monetary policy is a process where a central bank**

A     increases or decreases the supply of gilts

B     increase or decreases the value of loans to businesses

C     increases of decreases the rates of tax on businesses

D     increases or decreases the supply of money

**106   Tick if the following statements are true or false**

| Statement | True | False |
|---|---|---|
| The Bribery Act covers all aspects of white collar crime | | |
| Money laundering regulations only cover accountants | | |

# INTEREST RATES

**107   Which of the following best describes a capped rate of interest?**

A     Interest rate that is guaranteed not to exceed a specified level

B     Interest rate that remains the same for the period of borrowing

C     Interest charge that floats in line with bank base rates

D     Interest rate that fluctuates in line with an agreed indicator

**108** **Which of the following best describes a fixed rate of interest?**

    A     Interest rate that is guaranteed not to exceed a specified level

    B     Interest rate that remains the same for the period of borrowing

    C     Interest charge that floats in line with bank base rates

    D     Interest rate that fluctuates in line with an agreed indicator

**109** **Which of the following best describes a variable rate of interest?**

    A     Interest rate that is guaranteed not to exceed a specified level

    B     Interest rate that remains the same for the period of borrowing

    C     Interest charge that floats in line with bank base rates

    D     Interest rate that fluctuates in line with an agreed indicator

**110** **What does APR stand for?**

    A     Actual Percentage Rate

    B     Annual Percentage Rate

    C     Average Percentage Rate

    D     Annual Point Rate

**111** **Explain what APR is.**

# RAISING FINANCE

## FINANCING OPTIONS

**112** **Which one of the following best describes the main features of an overdraft?**

    A     Interest rates are low; it is available for as long as required; it is useful for capital purchases

    B     Interest rates are low; it is repayable on demand; it is useful for capital purchases

    C     Interest rates are low; repayments can be negotiated; it is useful for capital purchases

    D     Interest rates are high; repayments can be negotiated; It is a short-term form of finance

    E     Interest rates are high; it is repayable on demand; it is a short-term form of finance

    F     Interest rates are high; it is available for as long as required; it is a long-term form of finance

**113** Which one of the following best describes the main features of a bank loan?

A     Interest rates are low; it is available for as long as required; it is useful for capital purchases

B     Interest rates are low; it is repayable on demand; it is useful for capital purchases

C     Interest rates are low; repayments can be negotiated; it is useful for capital purchases

D     Interest rates are high; repayments can be negotiated; it is a short-term form of finance

E     Interest rates are high; it is repayable on demand; it is a short-term form of finance

F     Interest rates are high; it is available for as long as required; it is a long-term form of finance

**114** A bank has offered to lend a company £60,000 to be repaid over one year in equal monthly instalments of £5,500. **What is the flat rate of interest being charged?**

**115** **What is the annual flat rate of interest for a loan of £200,000 over 5 years if the monthly repayments are £4,000?**

**116** A bank has offered to lend a company £100,000 to be repaid over 36 months in equal instalments. The flat rate of interest is 2%.

**Calculate the monthly repayment of capital and interest to the nearest £.**

**117** A company has arranged a bank overdraft facility of £50,000. It has the following terms:

•     The current annual interest is 15%

•     The interest is calculated on the closing monthly overdrawn balance and is included in the next month's opening balance

•     Assume there are no differences in the monthly charges for the number of days in the month

**Calculate the monthly interest costs to the nearest penny. Minus signs must be used to denote any bank overdraft and interest to be paid**

|  | Month 3 | Month 4 | Month 5 | Month 6 | Month 7 |
|---|---|---|---|---|---|
| Forecast net cash flow | 7,500 | −7,500 | 15,000 | −15,000 | −10,000 |
| Opening balance | −5,000 |  |  |  |  |
| Closing balance before interest |  |  |  |  |  |
| Overdraft interest to be charged |  |  |  |  |  |

**118** A company invests £250,000 in shares of S Jack, a quoted company. S Jack has 20 million £1 shares in issue. The current market price of S Jack's share is £2.50. S Jack's operating profit in 20X2 was £15.41 million. The dividend paid to shareholders was 12p a share.

**Calculate the dividend yield for S Jack.**

**119** **Which of the following are types of security for borrowing?**

(i)     Floating charge

(ii)    Fixed charge

(iii)   Capped charge

(iv)    Variable charge

A      (i) and (ii)

B      (iii) and (iv)

C      (i), (ii) and (iv)

D      (ii) and (iv)

**120** **Identify whether the following statements are true or false**

| Statement | True | False |
|---|---|---|
| A floating charge is security on a loan supplied by a group of assets | | |
| A fixed charge is security on a loan supplied by a specific asset | | |

**121** **In times of increasing inflation which would be the best interest option when arranging a loan with a bank?**

A      Fixed rate

B      Variable rate

C      Semi-variable rate

**122** **Complete the sentences below by picking the correct options.**

A bank facility letter sets out the **[final/formal/legal/implied]** rights and duties of **[the bank/the customer/the bank and the customer]** when the bank grants **[an overdraft facility/a bank loan/an overdraft or a loan]**.

The purpose of a facility letter is to protect the rights of **[the bank/the customer/the bank and the customer]**.

A bank loan is often **[less/more]** expensive than an overdraft, mainly due to the **[higher/lower]** interest rates.

An overdraft can be **[more expensive/cheaper]** overall, because we only borrow what's needed, on a daily basis.

**123** The firm of Red & Bull is planning to expand its production facilities. The expansion plans will require the purchase of new machinery at a cost of £75,000 and a working capital injection of £34,000.

The partnership has been seeking possible means of funding the expansion and has been offered two options:

**Option 1**

A bank loan of £75,000 secured on the new machinery. Capital repayments are to be made over 3 years in equal, annual instalments. The interest rate is fixed at 8% per annum calculated on the capital balance outstanding at the beginning of each year.

An arrangement equal to 2% of the bank loan is payable at the beginning of the loan term.

The bank is also offering an overdraft facility up to £40,000 which attracts an annual interest rate of 20%. The partners believe that they will require an overdraft of £16,000 for nine months for the first year.

**Option 2**

A bank loan of £111,000 secured on the assets of the partnership. Principal (capital) repayments are to be made over 3 years, on a monthly basis.

The interest rate is fixed at 6% per annum for the first two years and will then revert to a variable interest rate set at 7% above the base rate. The interest charged is based on the amount outstanding at the start of each year.

An arrangement fee equal to 1% of the bank loan is payable at the beginning of the loan term.

Under this option there will be no requirement for a bank overdraft facility.

An extract from the partnership policy in respect of raising finance states the following:

- The maximum overdraft facility that the partnership may obtain is £20,000.
- Total costs are to be kept as low as possible.
- Loan finance may be secured on the assets of the partnership.
- The partners should not give personal guarantees or security for loan finance.

**Complete the table below to calculate the total cost to the partnership for the first two years of financing under each options:**

| | Loan interest £ | Capital repayments £ | Arrangement fee £ | Overdraft interest £ | Total cost £ |
|---|---|---|---|---|---|
| Option 1 | | | | | |
| Option 2 | | | | | |

**Based on these costs, and the partnership policy, which financing option should the partnership select? (Tick one.)**

| | |
|---|---|
| Option 1 | |
| Option 2 | |

124 Bogstandard Brooms is experiencing difficulty in collecting its debts within the terms of 30 days which they offer. Its sales ledger balances total, on average, £500,000 which is equivalent to 60 days sales. The company has an overdraft facility of £750,000 on which it pays interest of 8% per annum. Because of the high level of receivables, the overdraft level is never less than £500,000.

Cashrich Credit plc have offered them a without recourse factoring arrangement whereby they will administer the sales ledger, pay 85% of the invoice value immediately it is issued and the balance when they are paid by the customer or 60 days later, whichever is the earlier. They will charge 2½% of the revenue which is estimated at £3,000,000 per annum.

You estimate that this will save administration costs of the sales ledger of £15,000 per annum.

**Assuming that the customers will still pay after 60 days, will this be cost effective or not? Show your calculations.**

**125**

| Statement | True | False |
|---|---|---|
| Invoice discounting passes control of the sales ledger and credit control function to the invoice discounting company | | |

**126** A company needs to acquire some new plant and is considering the most appropriate means of funding the purchase. The purchase price is £400,000.

**Prepare notes describing the following financing options; include the implications of each option on:**

- the financial position of the company
- the gearing of the company
    1. Hire purchase agreement for 5 years
    2. Operating lease with a minimum term of 6 years
    3. Issue of equity shares
    4. Taking out a bank loan
    5. Funding using bonds
    6. Debt factoring

**127 Explain the differences between an operating lease and a finance lease.**

**128** A business requires a loan of £50,000 to re-equipment the machinery department.

There are 2 different loans available with different monthly repayment plans.

**Option 1**

- 1 payment of £2,500
- 60 payments of £800
- Final payment of £2,000

**Option 2**

- 1 payment of £2,500
- 30 payments of £1,750

**What is the interest cost of each option and which one should the business opt for?**

**129** A company intends to raise capital of £1.5 million to purchase a non-current asset. The following are option available to raise the finance required:

**Option 1**

- Bank loan of £1.5 million borrowed over 18 months
- Flat rate interest charged on the initial balance of 8%
- Arrangement fee of 2% of the initial loan payable in the first month

**Option 2**

- Hire purchase agreement for the non-current asset purchase of £1.5 million
- Total interest payable is £152,793
- 17 regular monthly payments
- Option to purchase in the last month at an extra cost of £91,836
- The term is 18 months with an APR of 12.5%

**Option 3**

- Operating Lease agreement for the non-current asset of £1.5 million
- Monthly payments will be £104,167

**What is the monthly and total cash flow of each option?**

130 A company wishes to borrow £300,000 to finance the purchase of new hi-tech printing machine. They expect to repay the borrowing over 90 months.

Three options have been identified.

| Option 1 | Bank loan repaid in 90 monthly instalments. Interest rate: 8.0% APR | Administration charge: £1,500 | Monthly repayment: £4,444 |
|---|---|---|---|
| Option 2 | Bank loan repaid in 30 equal quarterly instalments. Interest rate: 5.0% per annum flat rate. | Administration charge: £1,000 | |
| Option 3 | Bank overdraft facility of £300,000 which will be reviewed every year when the administration fee is paid. Interest rate: 11% per annum | Annual administration fee: £800 | |

In all options, the administration charge/fee is paid on the first day of the loan and if appropriate, on the anniversary of the loan and does not form part of the monthly repayment.

(a) **How much interest and administration charge will be paid is option 1 is taken?**

(b) **How much interest and administration charge will be paid if option 2 is taken?**

(c) **How much is the quarterly repayment for option 2?**

If option 3 is taken, the company expects to have an average overdraft of £150,000 over 7 and a half years. This amount should be used as the basis to calculate the interest charged on the overdraft.

(d) **How much interest and administration fee will be paid if option 3 is taken?**

**131**  A company's year end is 31$^{st}$ March 20X7

The company has taken out a 6 year bank loan on 30th September 20x5. The principle amount is £1,500,000 and is being repaid in equal monthly instalments.

In the year ending 31st March 20X6 £39,750 was paid in interest. In the year ending 31$^{st}$ March 20X7 £67,500 was paid in interest.

(a)  **Complete the accounting entry which would have been made on the day the loan was received.**

| Account | Debit | Credit | Amount £ |
|---|---|---|---|
| Current bank account | | | |
| Current loan account | | | |
| Long-term loan account | | | |

Below is the trial balance that will be used to prepare the company's financial statements as at 31$^{st}$ March 20X7

(b)  **Complete the missing figures. Round your answer to the nearest £000**

| Extract of the Trial balance | 31$^{st}$ March 20X7 | 31$^{st}$ March 20X6 |
|---|---|---|
| Plant and machinery | 8,000 | 6,300 |
| Inventories | 3,000 | 2,500 |
| Trade receivables | 2,100 | 2,100 |
| Bank current account | 60 | (60) |
| Trade payable | (5,700) | (5,100) |
| Other creditors | (1,900) | (1,600) |
| Current portion of long term loan | | |
| Long term loan | | |
| Retained profit | (4,900) | (3,300) |
| Share capital | (500) | (500) |
| | | |
| Turnover | (59,700) | (57,600) |
| Purchases | 43,600 | 42,700 |
| Other operating costs | 13,300 | 12,600 |
| Long term loan interest | | |
| Taxation | 1,200 | 1,200 |

(c)  **Calculate the gearing for both years. Round your answer to the nearest whole percent.**

| | 20X7 | 20X6 |
|---|---|---|
| Gearing | % | % |

**132** A company intends to raise capital of £1 million (£1m) to purchase a non-current asset. After considering many possibilities; they have narrowed their options down to the following:

**Option 1**

The company takes out a bank loan for £1m for two years, with interest chargeable at 6% per annum on the initial loan and an arrangement fee of 12.5% of the total interest payable on the loan. The agreed terms of the loan are that the interest is charged on a flat rate on the initial balance of £1m

**Option 2**

The company has a large balance of outstanding trade receivables and the credit control department is having little success in obtaining the outstanding debt from these customers. The company has been approached by a debt factoring company to purchase some of these trade receivables to the value of £1.25m from the company for £1m by entering into a factoring arrangement.

Rather than purchase the non-current asset, the company chooses to lease it instead. The lease will be treated as an operating lease and the lease rental payments will be £625,000 per annum.

**The finance director has asked you to prepare a report for each option, including the cost to the company together with its advantages and disadvantages. The report should also include the treatment of each option in the financial statements and how they affect the company's liquidity, gearing and credit rating.**

## INVESTING SURPLUS FUNDS

**133** KIT has £1 million to invest for one year. It can lock it away at a fixed rate of 7% for the full year, or invest at 6.5% for a three-month term, speculating on an increase in interest rates. Assume that the rate available increases to 7.5% after three months, and that KIT invests at this rate for the rest of the year.

**By how much is KIT better off from its gamble on interest rates?**

A    £2,500

B    £12,836

C    £73,414

D    £3,414

**134** A company has £500,000 surplus cash to be invested for 10 months only. There are two options available:

1    Place the money in a deposit account earning 3% interest per annum. There are no restrictions on withdrawal. Interest is paid annually on the anniversary of the opening of the account and on the day of closure of the account.

2    Place the money in a deposit account earning 5% interest per annum, providing the funds are not withdrawn before 12 months. The penalty of withdrawal is a loss of 3 months interest.

Answer the following questions based on the information

(a)   **How much interest is earned if option 1 is chosen?**

(b)   **How much interest is earned if option 2 is chosen?**

**135**   **Calculate the interest yield (to 2 decimal places) on 5.3% Treasury Stock 20X4 with a current market price of £105.**

**136**   An issue of 6% Treasury Stock 20X2 has taken place. The nominal value is £100. A company has purchased £150,000 worth of Gilts at a price of £175,000.

**Calculate how much interest the company will receive for each six month period and the interest yield (to two decimal places)**

**137**   A company has £800,000 invested in a one year fixed interest bond which pays 4.5% per annum. The company is going to have with draw the full amount from the investment in the 10$^{th}$ month of investment. The penalty for early redemption is the loss of one month's interest.

**Calculate the total amount of interest that the company will receive.**

**138**   **Explain THREE factors that a company should consider before deciding how to invest short term cash surpluses.**

**139**   A company invests £54,000 in a fixed interest deposit account for three years. The rate of interest is 8.6%.

**Calculate the balance in the account after three years if the interest is paid annually at the end of each year and the interest received remains in the account (to 2 decimal places).**

**140**   An investment has an interest rate of 2.9% above the base rate of 0.5%. **If £20,000 is invested what will be the value of the investment in one year's time?**

**141**   **How much will an investor need to invest for one year to earn £2,500 interest, assuming a fixed annual rate of interest of 2%?**

**142**   **Select the correct options to complete the following sentences:**

Certificates of deposit are certificates issued by **[banks/companies/stock exchange/local authority]** that certify that an amount of money has been deposited and will be repaid at a specific date in the future. They **[can/cannot]** be traded on a market. They are considered to be a **[low risk/high risk]** investment.

Local authority short-term loans are certificates issued by **[banks/companies/stock exchange/local authorities]** and backed by the government. They **[can/cannot]** be traded on a market. They are considered to be a **[low risk bank loan/high risk bank loan/low risk investment/high risk investment]**.

Government securities are also known as **[gold-edged/gilt-edged/gilted]** securities and **[can/cannot]** be traded. Interest rates are **[fixed/variable]** and these types of securities are considered to be **[low risk/high risk]** because they **[are/are not]** backed by the government.

Bank deposit accounts tend to have a **[lower/higher]** return than shares, as they are much **[lower/higher]** risk. They tend to have **[lower/higher]** interest rates than gilts and debentures as they are a **[more/less]** liquid investment.

Shares are issued by **[banks/companies/stock exchange/local authorities]** and **[can/cannot]** be traded. Dividends are usually **[fixed/variable]**. Shares are considered to be a **[low risk/high risk]** investment. This is because the returns from shares are **[fixed/sometime volatile]** and the value of the investment is **[stable/uncertain]**.

**143** A company has £9,000 to invest. It is going to buy 4% treasury stock. The interest receivable on the stock will be £600 in the year.

**What is the market price of the stock?**

**144** A company is going to make a dividend pay-out of £640,000. The share capital is £800,000 with a nominal value of £0.50 per share.

**What is the dividend payable per share?**

**145** A company is going to pay a dividend of £3 per share. The current market price is £30.50 per share.

**What is the dividend yield per share (2 decimal places)?**

**146** An investor bought 5,000 shares when the share price was £1.25 per share. The shares were sold eight months later at a gross profit of £750.

**What was the selling price per share?**

**147** The investment manual of a treasury department in a large company has the following policy for investing surplus funds:

- The investment must be convertible to cash within 45 days.
- The maximum amount to be invested in any one type of investment is £20,000.
- The interest rate must be at least 3% above base rate which is currently 1%.
- The investment must not include shares.
- Only low or medium risk investments are to be selected.

Four possible investment options are available:

**Option 1**

Investment of £20,000 required; 90 – day notice period; medium risk; investment portfolio includes shares; interest rate is 5% per annum.

**Option 2**

Maximum investment is £40,000 and minimum investment is £3,000; 30 – day notice period; interest rate is 4.5%; low risk; does not include investment in shares.

**Option 3**

Investment portfolio comprises stocks and shares; high risk; projected interest rate is 7% and a minimum investment of £40,000 is required; 40 – day notice period.

**Option 4**

Low risk; guaranteed return of 3% per annum; no stocks or shares; minimum investment of £52,000; 7–day notice period.

**Complete the table below, by typing either yes or no into each cell, to show which of the policy requirements are met by each of the options.**

| | Convertible within 45 days | Investment £20,000 or below | Interest rate 3% above base | Investment does not include shares | Low or Medium Risk |
|---|---|---|---|---|---|
| Option 1 | | | | | |
| Option 2 | | | | | |
| Option 3 | . | | | | |
| Option 4 | | | | | |

The company should select **[Option 1/Option 2/Option 3/Option 4/none of the options].**

**148** A company has surplus funds to invest for a period of 3 months. It is considering potential investment opportunities as follows:

**Investment 1**

Purchase treasury bills issued by the country's central bank. The treasury bills can be purchased now for a period of 91 days. The purchase price is £995 per £1,000.

**Investment 2**

Invest in a 30 day notice bank deposit account. The account will pay a variable rate of interest of 2.5% per annum, payable quarterly.

Compare and contrast the investment options. Your answer should include relevant calculations.

**149** DH raised cash through an equity share issue to pay for a new factory it planned to construct. However, the factory contract has been delayed and payments are not expected to be required for three or four months. DH is going to invest its surplus funds until they are required.

One of the directors of DH has identified three possible investment opportunities:

(i)    Treasury bills issued by the central bank of DH's country. They could be purchased on 1 December 20X6 for a period of 91 days. The likely purchase price is £990 per £1,000.

(ii)   Equities quoted on DH's local stock exchange. The stock exchange has had a good record in recent months with the equity index increasing in value for 14 consecutive months. The director recommends that DH invests in three large multinational entities, each paying an annual dividend that provides an annual yield of 10% on the current share price.

(iii)  DH's bank would pay 3.5% per year on money placed in a deposit account with 30 days' notice.

**Prepare notes on the risk and effective yield of each of the above investment opportunities.**

**150** The table below identifies the main features of four different investment opportunities:

| | Minimum investment | Maximum investment | Includes shares | Notice period | % return | Risk |
|---|---|---|---|---|---|---|
| Option 1 | £45,000 | £60,000 | Yes | 90 days | 3% variable | Medium |
| Option 2 | £25,000 | £75,000 | No | 30 days | 2% variable | Low |
| Option 3 | £30,000 | £100,000 | Yes | 40 days | 7% fixed | High |
| Option 4 | £53,000 | £70,000 | No | 7 days | 3.5% fixed | Low |

The general trend is that interest rates are decreasing and this trend is expected to continue for the foreseeable future.

**Identify which of the investment options are appropriate in each of the situation described below (there may be more than one suitable option)**

| | Suitable options |
|---|---|
| A partnership has £50,000 to invest | |
| An investing organisation requires a low risk investment | |
| A guaranteed interest rate of 3% is required | |
| The notice period needs to be less than 50 days | |
| The investment should not include shares | |

**151** A company has £250,000 surplus cash and the treasurer estimates that the cash is free to be invested for up to three years.

**Write a report which considers the risk, return and liquidity of each of the following investment options:**

- Land
- Long term bank deposit account
- Shares in a public company
- Certificates of deposit
- Treasury bills

**152** A company has £550,000 surplus cash to be invested.

**Discuss the option described below.**

**Option 1**

A four year fixed rate bond with a High Street bank paying interest of 6% per annum

**Option 2**

A business is looking to expand and is asking for help financing this expansion. The company is selling shares at £10 per share. The expansion will create new jobs in an area of unemployment.

**Option 3**

Invest in an oil mine. Shares are £15 each. Research shows that oil is in abundance but there are rumours of child labour and health and safety issue surrounding the mine's owners.

**153** The table below lists the assets in a portfolio of investments held by a company

| Investment | Value £000 | Expected return % |
|---|---|---|
| 1 | 1,500 | 5.0 |
| 2 | 5,000 | 8.0 |
| 3 | 1,000 | 2.5 |
| 4 | 750 | 1.2 |
| Total | 8,250 | |

(a) **Calculate the percentage expected return for the portfolio. Show your answer to one decimal place.**

The manager of the portfolio has cashed in investment 3.

(b) **Calculate the revised percentage expected return for the now reduced portfolio. Show you answer to one decimal place.**

**154** A company has £4,000,000 surplus cash to be invested for five years. The Finance Director has been tasked with preparing a board paper for discussion at the next board meeting. He has delegated this task to you as the Treasury Accountant.

The options are as follows:

1 A current account paying 0.4% interest per annum. Minimum investment £1.

2 A fixed rate account with a high street bank paying 2.4% interest per annum. Minimum investment £250,000.

3 A 90-day notice deposit account paying 1.1% interest per annum. Minimum investment £50,000.

4 Purchase 3% Treasury Stock with a redemption date in five years' time for the full £4,000,000 in £100 blocks. The nominal value of each block is £100.

5 Purchase £4,000,000 worth of Certificates of Deposit from a reputable UK bank in £1,000 blocks with an interest rate of 4% and a term of five years.

**Write a report to the Finance Director outlining the terms and conditions of each option together with the amount of income earned. Your answer should include brief comments on the risk, return and liquidity of each option and give a recommendation as to which option the company should select.**

# Section 2

# ANSWERS TO PRACTICE QUESTIONS

## CASH AND PROFIT

TYPES OF CASH FLOW

1

| Description | Type of receipt or payment |
|---|---|
| Proceeds from the disposal of non-current assets | Capital receipts |
| Buy new factory | Capital payment |
| Customer paying their debt | Regular revenue receipt |
| Pay legal fee due to product complaints | Exceptional payment |
| Unexpected tax refund | Exceptional receipt |
| Payment of wages | Regular revenue expense |
| Pay corporation tax for the year | Payment to HM Revenue and Customs |
| Payments made to the owners of the business | Drawings |

CASH ADJUSTMENTS

2   (a)   Trade receivables

| | £ | | £ |
|---|---|---|---|
| Opening balance | 10,500 | Cash received | 297,600 |
| Sales | 300,000 | Closing balance | 12,900 |
| | 310,500 | | 310,500 |

(b)   Rent

| | £ | | £ |
|---|---|---|---|
| Opening prepayment | 750 | Statement of profit or loss | 6,000 |
| Cash paid | 6,250 | Closing prepayment | 1,000 |
| | 7,000 | | 7,000 |

(c)    Payroll expenses

|  | £ |  | £ |
|---|---|---|---|
| Cash paid | 22,000 | Opening accrual | 200 |
| Closing accrual | 320 | Statement of profit or loss | 22,120 |
|  | 22,320 |  | 22,320 |

(d)    Trade payables

|  | £ |  | £ |
|---|---|---|---|
| Cash paid | 149,500 | Opening balance | 5,800 |
| Closing balance | 6,300 | Purchases | 150,000 |
|  | 155,800 |  | 155,800 |

**3      B**

|  | £ |
|---|---|
| Purchases on credit | 360,000 |
| Increase in trade payables | 15,000 |
| Therefore payments to suppliers | 345,000 |

An increase in trade payables means that the company is buying more on credit that they are paying back to their suppliers, for example:

**Trade payables**

|  | £ |  | £ |
|---|---|---|---|
| Cash paid | **345,000** | Opening balance | 6,000 |
| Closing balance 6,000 + 15,000 | 21,000 | Purchases | 360,000 |
|  | 366,000 |  | 366,000 |

Changes in inventory levels have no effect on expected cash payments.

**4      £15,900**

**Receivables**

|  | £ |  | £ |
|---|---|---|---|
| B/f | 70,000 | Returns | 2,000 |
| Sales | 200,000 | Cash | 250,000 |
|  |  | Irrecoverable debts (70,000 × 0.03) | 2,100 |
|  |  | C/f | 15,900 |
|  | 270,000 |  | 270,000 |

**5**     **£252,000**

|  | £ |
|---|---|
| Budgeted sales | 240,000 |
| Expected decrease in receivables | 12,000 |
|  | 252,000 |

The reduction in receivables means that the company will expect to receive more cash next month than the total of its credit sales for the month, for example:

**Trade receivables**

|  | £ |  | £ |
|---|---|---|---|
| Opening balance | 20,000 | Cash received | **252,000** |
| Sales | 240,000 | Closing balance 20,000 – 12,000 | 8,000 |
|  | 260,000 |  | 260,000 |

Changes in inventory levels have no effect on expected cash receipts.

**6**   (a)   **Disposals**

|  | £ |  | £ |
|---|---|---|---|
| Original cost | 12,000 | Accumulated depreciation | 5,250 |
|  |  | Loss on disposal | 1,750 |
|  |  | Cash received | 5,000 |
|  | 12,000 |  | 12,000 |

(b)   **Disposals**

|  | £ |  | £ |
|---|---|---|---|
| Original cost | 500 | Accumulated depreciation | 300 |
| Gain on disposal | 75 | Cash received | 275 |
|  | 575 |  | 575 |

(c)   **Disposals**

|  | £ |  | £ |
|---|---|---|---|
| Original cost | 12,000 | Accumulated depreciation | 5,856 |
|  |  | Loss on disposal | 2,644 |
|  |  | Part-exchange | 3,500 |
|  | 12,000 |  | 12,000 |

Total cost   – part-exchange value   = cash paid for new vehicle

13,500       – 3,500           = £10,000

**7**

|  | Workings | £ |
|---|---|---|
| Sales receipts | 3,520 + 51,000 – 12,400 | 42,120 |
| Purchases payments | 400 + 26,000 – 3,004 | 23,396 |
| Wages paid | As per SOPL | 12,900 |
| Advertising fees | 1,200 + 2,010 – 800 | 2,410 |
| Van expenses | 110 + 3,069 – 80 | 3,099 |
| Van depreciation | Non-cash | 0 |

**8**

|  | Workings | £ |
|---|---|---|
| Sales receipts | 13,520 + 351,000 – 31,000 | 333,520 |
| Purchases payments | 4,400 + 126,000 – 8,000 | 122,400 |
| Wages paid | As per SOPL | 32,900 |
| Electricity and van expenses paid | 1,200 + 22,010 + 23,069 – 2,100 | 44,179 |
| Phone expenses | 12,567 – 80 | 12,487 |

**9**

|  | Workings | £ |
|---|---|---|
| Rent paid | 12,650 – 1,200 – 1,200 | 10,250 |
| Office expenses | 370 + 6,640 – 441 | 6,569 |
| Printing expenses | 567 + 17,118 – 3,655 | 14,030 |

**10** (a) Calculate the cash received from receivables for the year ended 31 March 20x7.

|  | £ |  | £ |
|---|---|---|---|
| Credit sales | 29,200 | CASH | 25,800 |
|  |  | Balance c/f | 3,400 |
|  | 29,200 |  | 29,200 |

(b) Calculate the cash paid to payables for the year ended 31 March 20X7.

|  | £ |  | £ |
|---|---|---|---|
| CASH | 8,840 | Purchases | 11,200 |
| Discounts received | 1,165 |  |  |
| Balance c/f | 1,195 |  |  |
|  | 11,200 |  | 11,200 |

(c) Calculate the cash paid for rent for the year ended 31 March 20X7.

|  | £ |  | £ |
|---|---|---|---|
| CASH | 4,500 | Prepayment | 900 |
|  |  | Rent for the year | 3,600 |
|  | 4,500 |  | 4,500 |

(d)  Calculate the cash paid for general expenses for the year ended 31 March 20X7.

| | |
|---|---|
| 3 months' electricity = | £135 |
| Accrual needs to be for 2 months, therefore: | |
| Accrual = £135 × 2/3 = | £90 |
| | |
| General expenses | £1,840 |
| Less accrual | £90 |
| | |
| Cash | **£1,750** |

**11**

| | Workings | £ |
|---|---|---|
| Operating profit | | 10,520 |
| Change in inventory | £1,200 – £1,000 reduction in balance therefore increase in cash | 200 |
| Change in receivables | £10,000 – £7,650 reduction in balance therefore increase in cash | 2,350 |
| Change in payables | Closing balance = 1,200 + 2,400 – 2,000 = £1,600 £1,200 – £1,600 increase in balance therefore increase in cash | 400 |
| Adjustment for non-cash items | Depreciation charge | 250 |
| Purchase of non-current assets | £24,000 + £250 – £20,000 = £4,250 for additions | (4,250) |
| Tax paid | £2,600 + £2,700 – £2,800 = £2,500 paid | (2,500) |
| Net change in cash position | | 6,970 |
| Cash position 1 May | | 30,000 |
| Forecast cash position 31 July | | 36,970 |

**12**

| | Workings | £ |
|---|---|---|
| Operating profit | | 250,000 |
| Change in inventory | No change | 0 |
| Change in receivables | £108,000 – £100,000 increase in balance therefore reduction in cash | (8,000) |
| Change in payables | Closing balance = 50,000 + 200,000 – 230,000 = £20,000<br><br>£50,000 – £20,000 reduction in balance therefore reduction in cash | (30,000) |
| Adjustment for non-cash items | Depreciation charge | 25,000 |
| Purchase of non-current assets | £25,000 + £24,000 – £20,000 = £29,000 additions<br><br>£29,000 – £15,000 = £14,000 cash<br><br>£625 × 10 = £6,250 lease payments | (20,250) |
| Tax paid | £50,000 + £52,500 – £55,000 = £47,500 paid | (47,500) |
| Net change in cash position | | 169,250 |
| Cash position 1 January 20X6 | | 70,000 |
| Forecast cash position 31 December 20X6 | | 239,250 |

**13**

**Style Limited's Statement of profit or loss for the year ended 31 March 20X5**

| | £000 |
|---|---|
| Revenue | 8,210 |
| Cost of sales (W1) | (3,957) |
| | |
| Gross profit | 4,253 |
| Administrative expenses | (1,540) |
| Distribution costs | (1,590) |
| | |
| Operating profit | 1,123 |
| Finance cost (1,500 × 6%) | (90) |
| | |
| Profit before tax | 1,033 |
| Income tax expense (250 + 100) | (350) |
| | |
| Profit for the period | 683 |

**Workings:**

(W1)  **Cost of sales**

|  | £000 |
|---|---|
| Cost of goods | 3,463 |
| Add depreciation – buildings (W2) | 96 |
| – plant and equipment (W3) | 348 |
| Operating lease (W4) | 50 |
|  | 3,957 |

(W2)  **Buildings**

|  |  |
|---|---|
| Land and building at cost | 5,190 |
| Less: value of land | (2,000) |
|  | 3,190 |
| Depreciation for year 3,190 × 3% | 96 |

(W3)  **Plant and equipment**

|  |  |
|---|---|
| Plant and equipment cost | 3,400 |
| Less: Accumulated Depreciation | (1,659) |
|  | 1,741 |
| Depreciation for year 1,741 × 20% | 348 |

(W4)  **Operating lease**

|  |  |
|---|---|
| Total payments (4 × £62,500) | 250 |
| Allocated evenly over 5 periods (250/5) | 50 |

**14**

### Ruby and Daughters

### Statement of profit or loss for the year

|  | £ | £ |
|---|---|---|
| Sales (W1) |  | 44,000 |
| Opening inventory | 5,000 |  |
| Purchases (W2) | 23,000 |  |
| Less:  Closing inventory | (6,000) |  |
| Cost of sales |  | (22,000) |
| Gross profit |  | 22,000 |
| Wages and salaries | 20,800 |  |
| Rent (W3) | 4,700 |  |
| Sundry expenses (W4) | 250 |  |
| Depreciation (W5) | 10,000 |  |
|  |  | (35,750) |
| Net profit/(loss) |  | (13,750) |

**Workings:**

(W1)                    **Sales ledger control account**

| | £ | | £ |
|---|---|---|---|
| Opening balance | 12,000 | Cash received from customers | 40,000 |
| Sales | 44,000 | Closing balance | 16,000 |
| | ——— | | ——— |
| | 56,000 | | 56,000 |
| | ——— | | ——— |

(W2)                    **Purchase ledger control account**

| | £ | | £ |
|---|---|---|---|
| Payments made to suppliers | 25,000 | Opening balance | 7,000 |
| Closing balance | 5,000 | Purchases | 23,000 |
| | ——— | | ——— |
| | 30,000 | | 30,000 |
| | ——— | | ——— |

(W3)                    **Rent account**

| | £ | | £ |
|---|---|---|---|
| Bank account | 5,000 | Statement of profit or loss | 4,700 |
| | | Closing prepayment | 300 |
| | ——— | | ——— |
| | 5,000 | | 5,000 |
| | ——— | | ——— |

(W4)                    **Sundry expenses**

| | £ | | £ |
|---|---|---|---|
| Cash account | 200 | Statement of profit or loss | 250 |
| Closing accrual | 50 | | |
| | ——— | | ——— |
| | 250 | | 250 |
| | ——— | | ——— |

(W5) **Depreciation**

Depreciation charge (50,000 × 20%) = £10,000

| Debit | Depreciation expense (statement of profit or loss) | £10,000 |
|---|---|---|
| Credit | Accumulated depreciation (SFP) | £10,000 |

**15**

| Extract of the cash budget | Period 4 |
|---|---|
| | £000 |
| Receipts of cash sales | 760 × 10% = 76 |
| Receipts from trade receivables | 445 + (760 × 90%) − 423 = 706 |
| Receipt from disposal of non-current asset | 930 − 60 − 3 − 858 = 9 |
| Car lease payments | 6 + 13 − 15 = (14) |

# FORECASTING

## MOVING AVERAGES

**Note**: In the exam 'greyed out' boxes may no longer appear in which case zeros will need to be input to gain full marks.

**16** (a)

| | Sales volume (units) | Trend | Monthly variation |
|---|---|---|---|
| May | 61,600 | | |
| June | 39,100 | 52,000 | −12,900 |
| July | 55,300 | 55,500 | −200 |
| August | 72,100 | 59,000 | 13,100 |
| September | 49,600 | 62,500 | −12,900 |
| October | 65,800 | 66,000 | −200 |
| November | 82,600 | 69,500 | 13,100 |
| December | 60,100 | | |

(b)

| | Forecast trend | Variation | Forecast sales volume | Forecast sales £ | Forecast purchases £ |
|---|---|---|---|---|---|
| January | 76,500 | −200 | 76,300 | 1,106,350 | 331,905 |

**17** (a)

| | Sales volume (units) | Trend | Monthly variation |
|---|---|---|---|
| January | 19,906 | | |
| February | 22,390 | | |
| March | 20,555 | 20,570 | −15 |
| April | 18,666 | 20,620 | −1,954 |
| May | 21,333 | 20,670 | 663 |
| June | 20,156 | 20,720 | −564 |
| July | 22,640 | 20,770 | 1,870 |
| August | 20,805 | 20,820 | −15 |
| September | 18,916 | 20,870 | −1,954 |
| October | 21,583 | | |
| November | 20,406 | | |

(b)

| | Forecast trend | Variation | Forecast sales volume | Forecast sales £ | Forecast purchases £ |
|---|---|---|---|---|---|
| December | 21,020 | 1,870 | 22,890 | 686,700 | 192,276 |

**18** (a)

| | Sales volume (units) | Trend | Monthly variation % (2 d.p.) |
|---|---|---|---|
| October | 6,408 | | |
| November | 8,816 | 8,303 | 106.18% or 6.18% |
| December | 9,686 | 8,479 | 114.24% or 14.24% |
| January | 6,934 | 8,713 | 79.58% or −20.42% |
| February | 9,520 | 8,965 | 106.19% or 6.19% |
| March | 10,440 | 9,140 | 114.22% or 14.22% |
| April | 7,460 | 9,375 | 79.57% or −20.43% |
| May | 10,225 | | |

**Note:** In the exam it will be clear which answer is required.

(b) The average monthly trend (to the nearest whole number) is [ 214 ]

**19** (a)

| | |
|---|---|
| Sales of footballs increase when the world cup is on. | |
| Sales of greetings cards increase in December. | ✓ |
| Sales of milk remain constant all year. | |
| Sales of houses increase in Spring. | ✓ |
| Sales of newspapers rise whenever it rains. | |

(b)

| | |
|---|---|
| Tennis rackets sales increase during Wimbledon. | |
| Over summer, more hosepipes are sold. | |
| Sales of raincoats increase in April. | |
| During the last general election, sales of ice-cream increased. | |
| Sales of diet books reach a peak after every Olympics. | ✓ |

(c) A seasonal variation is a change in sales which occurs **at regular intervals, normally of less than a year** whereas a cyclical variation occurs **over a long time period.**

The underlying sales trend is the sales level excluding **all variations**.

**20** (a)

| | |
|---|---|
| Sales of houses increase when the England cricket team wins. | |
| Sales of wrapping paper increase in November and December. | ✓ |
| Sales of venetian blinds have been falling consistently for 3 years. | |
| Sales of wallpaper increase at the same time that sales of toothpaste fall. | |
| Sales of shoes rise in the summer. | ✓ |

(b)

| | |
|---|---|
| Tennis rackets sales decrease when it rains. | |
| Over summer, more ice creams are sold. | |
| Sales of gloves increase in Autumn. | |
| When Sky HD was launched a carpet firm in Cardiff experienced 20% sales growth. | |
| Over the last 50 years the average price of oil has increased for 5 years, then decreased for 5 years. This pattern continued over the 50 year period. | ✓ |

## MARK-UP AND MARGIN

**21**  (a)  £900/100 × 140 = £1,260

(b)  £900/60 × 100 = £1,500

**22**  (a)

| | Sales volume (units) | Trend | Monthly variation |
|---|---|---|---|
| February | 10,100 | | |
| March | 10,950 | 10,900 | 50 |
| April | 11,650 | 11,200 | 450 |
| May | 11,000 | 11,500 | −500 |
| June | 11,850 | 11,800 | 50 |
| July | 12,550 | 12,100 | 450 |
| August | 11,900 | 12,400 | −500 |
| September | 12,750 | | |

The monthly variation in July is **450** units.

(b)

| | Forecast trend | Variation | Forecast sales volume | Forecast sales £ |
|---|---|---|---|---|
| October | 13,000 | 450 | 13,450 | 289,175 |

(c)  £289,175 × 80% = £231,340

(d)  £289,175/125 × 100 = £231,340

**23**

| | Manufacturing | Sales | External |
|---|---|---|---|
| *20X0* | | | |
| January | 230 | × 1.05 = 241.50 | × 1.1 = 265.65 |
| February | 140 | × 1.05 = 147.00 | × 1.1 = 161.70 |
| March | 132 | × 1.05 = 138.60 | × 1.1 = 152.46 |
| | | | |
| January | 51 | n/a | ÷ 93 × 100 = 54.84 |
| February | 60 | n/a | ÷ 93 × 100 = 64.52 |
| March | 18 | n/a | ÷ 93 × 100 = 19.35 |
| | | Total monthly sales value | 718.52 |

## INDEXING

**24**

| Month | 1 | 2 | 3 | 4 | 5 | 6 | 7 |
|---|---|---|---|---|---|---|---|
| Price | 0.12 | 0.15 | 0.21 | 0.32 | 0.26 | 0.25 | 0.30 |
| Index | 57.14 | 71.43 | 100 | 152.38 | 123.8 | 119.05 | 142.86 |

Month 1 = 0.12 ÷ 0.21 × 100 = 57.14

Month 7 = 0.30 ÷ 0.21 × 100 = 142.86

**25  C**

£20,500 ÷ 131 × 151 = £23,630

**26  C**

Current cost = £5 × 430 ÷ 150

**27  A**

(£2,000 × 120 ÷ 160) = £1,500

**28**  (a)

| Period | 1 | 2 | 3 | 4 | 5 |
|---|---|---|---|---|---|
| Sales price (£) | 40.00 | 55.00 | 40/80×120 = 60.00 | 48.00 | 40/80×121= 60.50 |
| Index | 80.00 | 80/40×55 = 110.00 | 120.00 | 80/40×48 = 96.00 | 121.00 |

(b)  40.00 ÷ 100 × 80 = £32.00

**29**  (a)

| Month | Purchases volume (tonnes) | Trend | Monthly variation |
|---|---|---|---|
| 1 | 5,150 | | |
| 2 | 5,241 | 5,293 | −52 |
| 3 | 5,487 | 5,448 | 39 |
| 4 | 5,615 | 5,461 | 154 |
| 5 | 5,280 | 5,450 | −170 |
| 6 | 5,456 | 5,461 | −5 |
| 7 | 5,648 | 5,665 | −17 |
| 8 | 5,890 | 5,662 | 228 |
| 9 | 5,448 | 5,676 | −228 |
| 10 | 5,689 | 5,661 | 28 |
| 11 | 5,847 | 5,845 | 2 |
| 12 | 6,000 | | |

(b)  (5,845 – 5,293) ÷ 9 = 61 tonnes

(c)

| Month 17 (tonnes) | Month 18 (tonnes) |
|---|---|
| 6,211 | 6,272 |

(d)  6,272 × £56 × 142 ÷ 125 = £398,999.55 = £399,000 rounded

## REGRESSION ANALYSIS

**30**  Orders = 100,000 + (30 × 240) = 107,200

Orders adjusted for seasonal index = [100,000 + (30 × 240)] × 1.08 = 115,776

Overhead cost = £10,000 + (£0.25 × 115,776) = £38,944

Answer is £39,000

**31**  We have been given the trend equation. We need to plug in the value for x so that we can find y.

X is the time period reference number and for the first quarter of year 1 is 1. The time period reference number for the third quarter of year 7 is 27. (Just keep adding 1 to the time period reference number for each new quarter, thus quarter 2, year 1, x = 2; quarter 3, year 1, x = 3; quarter 4, year 1, x = 4; quarter 1, year 2, x = 5, etc.)

y = 25,000 + 6,500 × 27 = 200,500 units

This is the trend we now need to multiply by the seasonal variation for quarter 3:

Forecast = 200,500 × 150/100 = 300,750 units.

**32**  **D**

| Quarter | Value of x | | Trend units | | | Forecast sales units |
|---|---|---|---|---|---|---|
| 1 | 25 | y = (26 × 25) + 8,850 | 9,500 | × 85% | = | 8,075 |
| 2 | 26 | y = (26 × 26) + 8,850 | 9,526 | × 95% | = | 9,050 |
| 3 | 27 | y = (26 × 27) + 8,850 | 9,552 | × 105% | = | 10,030 |
| 4 | 28 | y = (26 × 28) + 8,850 | 9,578 | × 115% | = | 11,015 |
| | | | | | | ——— |
| | | | | | | 38,170 |
| | | | | | | ——— |

Difference between Q1 and Q4 budgeted sales = 11,015 – 8,075 = 2,940 units

**33**  **D**

Since no inventories are held, budgeted production will be equal to budgeted sales.

Budgeted production each quarter = 38,170/4 = 9,542.5 units

**34**

| Quarter | Trend sales units | Actual sales units | Variation units |
|---------|------------------|--------------------|-----------------|
| 1 | 13,000 | 14,000 | +1,000 |
| 2 | 16,000 | 18,000 | +2,000 |
| 3 | 19,000 | 18,000 | −1,000 |
| 4 | 22,000 | 20,000 | −2,000 |

Year 2 Quarter 1 = 10,000 + (3,000 × 5) = 25,000 + 1,000 = 26,000 units

Year 2 Quarter 2 = 10,000 + (3,000 × 6) = 28,000 + 2,000 = 30,000 units

Year 2 Quarter 3 = 10,000 + (3,000 × 7) = 31,000 − 1,000 = 30,000 units

Year 2 Quarter 4 = 10,000 + (3,000 × 8) = 34,000 − 2,000 = 32,000 units

**35** (a)

| Year | Actual Overheads | Cost index | Adjustment factor | Costs at 20Y1 price level |
|------|-----------------|------------|-------------------|---------------------------|
| | £ | | | £ |
| 20X8 | 143,040 | 192 | × 235/192 | 175,075 |
| 20X9 | 156,000 | 200 | × 235/200 | 183,300 |
| 20Y0 | 152,320 | 224 | × 235/224 | 159,800 |
| 20Y1 | 172,000 | 235 | × 235/235 | 172,000 |

(b) If the forecast number of machine hours is 3,100 and the cost index is 250:

Forecast overhead costs = [£33,000 + (£47 × 3,100 hours)] × (250/235)

= £178,700 × (250/235)

= £190,106

**36** C = F + Vx

14,520 = 7,788 + V(3,300)

6,732 = 3,300V

V = 2.04

## PATTERNS OF CASH FLOW

### CASH RECEIPTS

**37** (i)

|  | | April £ | May £ | June £ |
|---|---|---|---|---|
| Sales | | 20,000 | 20,400 | 20,808 |
| Cash receipts | (40%) | 8,000 | 8,160 | 8,323 |
| Credit sales | (60%) | 12,000 | 12,240 | 12,485 |
| Receipts from receivables (30%) | | | 3,600 | 3,672 |
| | (65%) | | | 7,800 |
| | Total cash receipts for June | | | 19,795 |

(ii)

|  | £ |
|---|---|
| Opening receivables | 0 |
| Total sales | 61,208 |
| Total receipts | −39,555 |
| Closing receivables | 21,653 |

(iii)   £12,240 × 5% = £612

**38**

|  | June | July | August | September |
|---|---|---|---|---|
| Sales (units) | | 5,000 | 4,000 | 4,400 |
| £ per unit | | 60 | 65 | 65 |
| Total sales | | 300,000 | 260,000 | 286,000 |
| Credit sales (sales units − 2,500 units) × £ per unit | 103,500 | 150,000 | 97,500 | 123,500 |
| | | | | |
| Cash sales (2,500 units × £ per unit) | | 150,000 | 162,500 | 162,500 |
| In month (credit sales × 60% × 98%) | | 88,200 | 57,330 | 72,618 |
| Month following (credit sales × 40%) | | 41,400 | 60,000 | 39,000 |
| Cash receipts | | 279,600 | 279,830 | 274,118 |

**39** (a)

|  | March £ | April £ | May £ | June £ |
|---|---|---|---|---|
| Monthly credit sales receipts | 59,156 | 61,272 | 54,786 | 69,212 |

**Workings:**

|  | January | February | March | April | May | June |
|---|---|---|---|---|---|---|
| Total sales | 61,000 | 72,000 | 54,000 | 72,500 | 81,600 | 92,000 |
| Credit sales 92% | 56,120 | 66,240 | 49,680 | 66,700 | 75,072 | 84,640 |
| 1 month after sale |  | 16,836 | 19,872 | 14,904 | 20,010 | 22,522 |
| 2 months after sale |  |  | 39,284 | 46,368 | 34,776 | 46,690 |
| Total credit receipts |  |  | 59,156 | 61,272 | 54,786 | 69,212 |

(b) The trade receivables balance at the end of June is forecast to be £137,190

**Workings:**

| All June credit sales outstanding = 92,000 × 92% | = £84,640 |
|---|---|
| 70% May credit sales outstanding = 81,600 × 92% × 70% | = £52,550 |
| Total outstanding | = £137,190 |

**40** (a) **C**

| March total sales × 15% | £6,600 |
|---|---|
| February total sales × 85% × 60% | £31,620 |
| January total sales × 85% × 40% | £17,340 |
| Total | £55,560 |

(b) The trade receivables balance at the end of March is forecast to be £58,480

**Workings:**

| All March credit sales outstanding = £44,000 × 85% | = £37,400 |
|---|---|
| 40% February credit sales outstanding = £62,000 × 85% × 40% | = £21,080 |
| Total outstanding | = £58,480 |

**41**

|  | April | May |
|---|---|---|
| Total sales receipts £ | 378 | 391 |

The trade receivables balance at the end of May is forecast to be £343.

**42**

|  | April £ | May £ |
|---|---|---|
| Total sales receipts | 14,175 | 17,985 |

The trade receivables balance at the end of May is forecast to be £24,140.

**43**

| | April | May | June |
|---|---|---|---|
| Cash sales | 15,000 | 15,000 | 15,000 |
| Credit sales receipts | 146,500 | 164,400 | 200,475 |
| Total receipts | 161,500 | 179,400 | 215,475 |

**Workings:**

Cash sales = 5,000 × £3 = £15,000

Credit sales:

| | April £ | May £ | June £ |
|---|---|---|---|
| Credit sales | 198,000 | 206,250 | 214,500 |
| Receipts | | | |
| February credit sales | 101,500 | | |
| March credit sales | 45,000 | 105,000 | |
| April credit sales | | 59,400 | 138,600 |
| May credit sales | | | 61,875 |
| Total credit sales receipts | 146,500 | 164,400 | 200,475 |

**44**

| | October | November | December |
|---|---|---|---|
| Cash sales (50%) | 300,000 | 340,000 | 450,000 |
| Credit sales receipts | 300,000 | 300,000 | 340,000 |
| Total cash received | 600,000 | 640,000 | 790,000 |

**Workings:**

Total sales

September = 20,000 × £30 = £600,000

October = 15,000 × £40 = £600,000

November = 17,000 × £40 = £680,000

December = 18,000 × £50 = £900,000

Credit sales:

| | September £ | October £ | November £ | December £ |
|---|---|---|---|---|
| Credit sales (50%) | 300,000 | 300,000 | 340,000 | 450,000 |
| Receipts | | | | |
| September credit sales | | 300,000 | | |
| October credit sales | | | 300,000 | |
| November credit sales | | | | 340,000 |

**45**

|  | July | August | September |
|---|---|---|---|
| Credit sales receipts | 10,156 | 11,349 | 10,599 |

Workings:

|  | April £ | May £ | June £ | July £ | August £ | September £ |
|---|---|---|---|---|---|---|
| Credit sales | 9,375 | 12,000 | 10,015 | 11,365 | 10,800 | 12,495 |

|  | July £ | August £ | September £ |
|---|---|---|---|
| Receipts |  |  |  |
| April credit sales | 3,750 |  |  |
| May credit sales | 2,400 | 4,800 |  |
| June credit sales | 4,006 | 2,003 | 4,006 |
| July credit sales |  | 4,546 | 2,273 |
| August credit sales |  |  | 4,320 |
| Total credit sales receipts | 10,156 | 11,349 | 10,599 |

**46**

|  | Cash receipts | £ |
|---|---|---|
| Month 4 | £108,000 × 20% | 21,600 |
| Month 3 | £120,000 × 80% × 40% × 0.985 | 37,824 |
| Month 2 | £105,000 × 80% × 30% | 25,200 |
| Month 1 | £90,000 × 80% × 28% | 20,160 |
|  | Total receipts | 104,784 |

## CASH PAYMENTS

**47**

| Skilled |  | £ |
|---|---|---|
| Product A | 1,750 units × 2 hours/unit × £10/hour | 35,000 |
| Product B | 5,000 units × 2 hours/unit × £10/hour | 100,000 |
|  |  |  |
| Unskilled |  |  |
| Product A | 1,750 units × 3 hours/unit × £7/hour | 36,750 |
| Product B | 5,000 units × 4 hours/unit × £7/hour | 140,000 |
|  |  |  |
|  |  | 311,750 |

**48    D**

Paid hours including idle time = 2,400 × 100/80 = 3,000

Budgeted labour cost = 3,000 hours × £10 = £30,000

**49**

|  | April £ | May £ |
|---|---|---|
| Settlement of trade payable | 2,320 | 2,000 |

**50** (a)

|  | £ |
|---|---|
| Opening balance | 0 |
| Purchase July to September | 17,250 |
| Payments July to September | 7,800 |
| Closing balance | 9,450 |

(b)

|  | October £ | November £ |
|---|---|---|
| Purchases | 5,850 | 6,100 |

**Workings:**

|  | July £ | August £ | September £ | October £ | November £ | December £ |
|---|---|---|---|---|---|---|
| Purchases | 5,500 | 5,750 | 6,000 | 6,250 | 6,500 | 6,750 |
| 1 month after purchase |  | 2,200 | 2,300 | 2,400 | 2,500 | 2,600 |
| 2 months after purchase |  |  | 3,300 | 3,450 | 3,600 | 3,750 |

**51** (a)

|  | April £ | May £ |
|---|---|---|
| Settlement of trade payables | 14,880 | 9,120 |

**Workings**

|  |  | £ |
|---|---|---|
| April: | All of January's outstanding balance | 5,280 |
|  | February £8,640 ÷ 60 × 20 | 2,880 |
|  | March £16,800 × 40% | 6,720 |
|  | Total | 14,880 |
| May: | February £8,640 ÷ 60 × 40 | 5,760 |
|  | March £16,800 × 20% | 3,360 |
|  | Total | 9,120 |

(b)

| | January £ | February £ | March £ | April £ | May £ |
|---|---|---|---|---|---|
| Expenses | 4,512 | 4,951 | 5,541 | 5,745 | 6,785 |
| Total cost to be included in cash budget | 23,512 | 23,951 | 24,541 | 4,745 | 5,785 |

Monthly depreciation = £60,000 × 20% = £12,000 ÷ 12 = £1,000

Purchase of machine = £60,000 ÷ 3 = £20,000

**52**

| | October £000 | November £000 | December £000 |
|---|---|---|---|
| Trade payables | 120 | 120 | 120 |
| Direct labour | 210 | 210 | 560 |
| Administration cost | 60 | 60 | 60 |
| Production costs | 105 | 105 | 280 |
| Distribution costs | 21 | 21 | 56 |
| Non-current asset purchase | 300 | 25 | – |
| **Total payments** | **816** | **541** | **1,076** |

**Workings:**

| | September | October | November | December |
|---|---|---|---|---|
| Sales units 000s | 20 | 15 | 15 | 15 |
| Production units 000s | 15 | 15 | 15 | 40 |
| Purchase value £000 | 15 × 8 = 120 | 15 × 8 = 120 | 15 × 8 = 120 | 40 × 8 = 320 |
| Payments £000 | | 120 | 120 | 120 |
| Labour £000 | | 15 × 2 × 7 = 210 | 15 × 2 × 7 = 210 | 40 × 2 × 7 = 560 |
| Admin £000 | | 90 − 30 = 60 | 90 − 30 = 60 | 90 − 30 = 60 |
| Production £000 | | 15 × (10 − 3) = 105 | 15 × (10 − 3) = 105 | 40 × (10 − 3) = 280 |
| Distribution £000 | | 210 × 10% = 21 | 210 × 10% = 21 | 560 × 10% = 56 |

**53   B**

| | May £ |
|---|---|
| Purchases | 124,000 × 42% = 52,080 |
| Wages | 8,100 |
| Expenses | 12,200 |
| New machine | 39,000 ÷ 3 = 13,000 |
| **Total payments** | **85,380** |

**54**

|  | April £ | May £ |
|---|---|---|
| Supervisor | 1,800 | 1,800 |
| Standard hours | 23,400 | 22,200 |
| Overtime | 2,250 | 2,550 |
| **Total labour costs** | 27,450 | 26,550 |

**55**

|  | Period 10 £ | Period 11 £ | Period 12 £ |
|---|---|---|---|
| Current terms | 304,500 | 308,250 | 312,750 |
| Competitor terms | 329,000 | 207,000 | 214,000 |
| Option 1 | 400,200 | 270,600 | 290,400 |
| Option 2 | 412,050 | 292,575 | 299,625 |

**Workings:**

**Current terms**

|  | 10 | 11 | 12 |
|---|---|---|---|
| Period of purchase | £31,500 | £30,750 | £33,000 |
| Period following purchase | £150,000 | £157,500 | £153,750 |
| 2 periods following purchase | £123,000 | £120,000 | £126,000 |
| **Total** | **£304,500** | **£308,250** | **£312,750** |

**Competitor terms**

|  | 10 | 11 | 12 |
|---|---|---|---|
| Period of purchase | £126,000 | £123,000 | £132,000 |
| Period following purchase | £80,000 | £84,000 | £82,000 |
| 2 periods following purchase | £123,000 | £0 | £0 |
| **Total** | **£329,000** | **£207,000** | **£214,000** |

**Option 1**

|  | 10 | 11 | 12 |
|---|---|---|---|
| Period of purchase | £277,200 | £270,600 | £290,400 |
| Period following purchase | £0 | £0 | £0 |
| 2 periods following purchase | £123,000 | £0 | £0 |
| **Total** | **£400,200** | **£270,600** | **£290,400** |

**Option 2**

|  | 10 | 11 | 12 |
|---|---|---|---|
| Period of purchase | £148,050 | £144,525 | £155,100 |
| Period following purchase | £141,000 | £148,050 | £144,525 |
| 2 periods following purchase | £123,000 | £0 | £0 |
| **Total** | **£412,050** | **£292,575** | **£299,625** |

**56**

|  | July £000 | August £000 | September £000 | October £000 |
|---|---|---|---|---|
| Sales | 100 | 90 | 125 | 140 |
| Cost of sales (sales/125 × 100) | 80 | 72 | 100 | 112 |
| Opening inventory | 40 | 36 | 50 | 56 |
| Closing inventory* | 36 | 50 | 56 |  |
| Purchase (cost of sale – opening + closing) | 76 | 86 | 106 |  |
| Paid |  | (i) 76 | (ii) 86 | (iii) 106 |

*Closing inventory = 0.5 × Following month's cost of sales

**57**

|  | July £ | August £ |
|---|---|---|
| April collected | 6,000 | 0 |
| May collected | 19,200 × 50 ÷ 80 = 12,000 | 19,200 × 30 ÷ 80 = 7,200 |
| June | 28,400 × 20% = 5,680 | 28,400 × 50% = 14,200 |
| Settlement of trade payables | 23,680 | 21,400 |

**58**

(a)

| Month | July | August | September | October |
|---|---|---|---|---|
| Total payment | Standard 340,000 × 80% = 272,000 | Standard 360,000 × 80% = 288,000 | Standard 350,000 × 80% = 280,000 | Standard 400,000 × 80% = 320,000 |
|  | Overtime = 90,000 | Overtime = 340,000 × 20% = 68,000 | Overtime = 360,000 × 20% = 72,000 | Overtime = 350,000 × 20% = 70,000 |
|  | NIC = 32,000 | NIC Standard = 272,000 × 10% = 27,200 | NIC Standard = 288,000 × 10% = 28,800 | NIC Standard = 280,000 × 10% = 28,000 |
|  | **Total £394,000** | NIC Overtime = 90,000 × 12% = 10,800 | NIC Overtime = 68,000 × 12% 8,160 | NIC Overtime = 72,000 × 12% = 8,640 |
|  |  | **Total £394,000** | Bonus = £125,000 | NIC Bonus = 125,000 × 12% = 15,000 |
|  |  |  | **Total £513,960** | **Total £441,640** |

(b)    400,000 × 20% × 12% = **£9,600**

# CASH BUDGETS

**59** (a)

|  | June | July | August |
|---|---|---|---|
|  | £ | £ | £ |
| Material usage | 8,000 | 9,000 | 10,000 |
| Less: Opening inventory | 5,000 | 3,500 | 6,000 |
| Closing inventory | 3,500 | 6,000 | 4,000 |
|  |  |  |  |
| Purchases | 6,500 | 11,500 | 8,000 |

(b) Cash budgets, June – August

|  | June | July | August |
|---|---|---|---|
|  | £ | £ | £ |
| **Receipts of cash** |  |  |  |
| Cash sales | 4,500 | 5,000 | 6,000 |
| Credit sales | 29,500 | 40,500 | 45,000 |
|  |  |  |  |
|  | 34,000 | 45,500 | 51,000 |
|  |  |  |  |
| **Cash payments** |  |  |  |
| Wages | 12,000 | 13,000 | 14,500 |
| Overheads | 6,500 | 7,000 | 8,000 |
| Direct materials | 6,500 | 11,500 | 8,000 |
| Taxation | – | 25,000 | – |
|  |  |  |  |
|  | 25,000 | 56,500 | 30,500 |
|  |  |  |  |
| Surplus/(deficit) for month | 9,000 | (11,000) | 20,500 |
| Opening balance | 11,750 | 20,750 | 9,750 |
|  |  |  |  |
| Closing balance | 20,750 | 9,750 | 30,250 |

(c) Cash budgets are an important part of business planning. They highlight future surpluses of cash (enabling managers to make appropriate plans for investing the surplus) and shortfalls of cash (enabling managers to take appropriate action in advance, perhaps by advising their bank of overdraft requirements or raising funds from other sources).

**60** Cash flow forecast for the three months ended 30 September 2006

|  | July £ | Aug £ | Sept £ |
|---|---|---|---|
| **Receipts** |  |  |  |
| From receivables (W1) | 10,250 | 11,125 | 12,237 |
| **Payments** |  |  |  |
| To payables (W2) | 5,100 | 5,559 | 6,059 |
| Packing costs | 1,800 | 1,800 | 1,800 |
| Sundry expenses | 800 | 800 | 800 |
| Total | 7,700 | 8,159 | 8,659 |
| Net cash flow | 2,550 | 2,966 | 3,578 |
| Balance brought forward | −6,000 | −3,450 | −484 |
| Balance carried forward | −3,450 | −484 | 3,094 |

**Workings:**

(W1) **Receipts from receivables**

|  | May £ | June £ | July £ | Aug £ | Sept £ |
|---|---|---|---|---|---|
| **Sales** | 10,000 | 10,000 | 11,000 | 12,100 | 13,310 |
| **Receipts** |  |  |  |  |  |
| May | 2,500 | 6,000 | 1,500 |  |  |
| June |  | 2,500 | 6,000 | 1,500 |  |
| July |  |  | 2,750 | 6,600 | 1,650 |
| Aug |  |  |  | 3,025 | 7,260 |
| Sept |  |  |  |  | 3,327 |
|  |  |  | 10,250 | 11,125 | 12,237 |

(W2) **Payments to payables**

€7,080 × 0.7203 = £5,099.724 rounded to the nearest £ = £5,100

|  | May £ | June £ | July £ | Aug £ | Sept £ |
|---|---|---|---|---|---|
| **Purchase** | 5,100 | 5,100 | 5,559 | 6,059 | 6,604 |
| Paid next month |  |  | 5,100 | 5,559 | 6,059 |

**61**

| | June £ | July £ | August £ |
|---|---|---|---|
| **RECEIPTS** | | | |
| Cash sales | 1,100 | 1,200 | 2,300 |
| Credit sales | 40,810 | 60,540 | 70,990 |
| Bank loan | 0 | 30,000 | 0 |
| **Total receipts** | 41,910 | 91,740 | 73,290 |
| **Payments** | | | |
| Purchases | −42,111 | −20,804 | −41,305 |
| Wages | −18,000 | −11,000 | −12,100 |
| Expenses | −2,555 | −1,543 | −1,100 |
| Capital expenditure | 0 | 0 | −2,000 |
| Bank loan repayment | 0 | 0 | −3,240 |
| Overdraft interest | −100 | −517 | 0 |
| **Total payments** | −62,766 | −33,864 | −59,745 |
| Net cash flow | −20,856 | 57,876 | 13,545 |
| Opening bank balance | −5,000 | −25,856 | 32,020 |
| **Closing bank balance** | −25,856 | 32,020 | 45,565 |

**62**

| | April £ | May £ | June £ |
|---|---|---|---|
| **RECEIPTS** | | | |
| Cash sales | 8,100 | 8,400 | 9,150 |
| Credit sales | 26,690 | 29,550 | 32,850 |
| Bank loan | 100,000 | 0 | 0 |
| **Total receipts** | 134,790 | 37,950 | 42,000 |
| **PAYMENTS** | | | |
| Purchases | −15,600 | −16,224 | −16,873 |
| Wages | −8,000 | −8,000 | −8,000 |
| Expenses | −4,750 | −4,950 | −5,125 |
| Tax payment | −60,000 | 0 | 0 |
| Bank loan repayment | 0 | −5,050 | −5,050 |
| Overdraft interest | 0 | 0 | 0 |
| **Total payments** | −88,350 | −34,224 | −35,048 |
| Net cash flow | 46,440 | 3,726 | 6,952 |
| Opening bank balance | 50,000 | 96,440 | 100,166 |
| **Closing bank balance** | 96,440 | 100,166 | 107,118 |

**Workings:**

|  | April<br>£ | May<br>£ | June<br>£ |
|---|---|---|---|
| Cash sales | 40,500 × 20% = 8,100 | 42,000 × 20% = 8,400 | 45,750 × 20% = 9,150 |

|  | April<br>£ | May<br>£ | June<br>£ |
|---|---|---|---|
| Credit sales: |  |  |  |
| From February | 32,500 × 50% = 16,250 |  |  |
| From March | 34,800 × 30% = 10,440 | 34,800 × 50% = 17,400 |  |
| From April |  | 40,500 × 30% = 12,150 | 40,500 × 50% = 20,250 |
| From May |  |  | 42,000 × 30% = 12,600 |
| Total credit sales receipts | 26,690 | 29,550 | 32,850 |

|  | February<br>£ | March<br>£ | April<br>£ | May<br>£ | June<br>£ |
|---|---|---|---|---|---|
| Credit purchases | 15,000 | 15,000 × 1.04<br>= 15,600 | 15,600 × 1.04<br>= 16,224 | 16,224 × 1.04<br>= 16,873 | 16,873 × 1.04<br>= 17,548 |
| Purchase payments |  | 15,000 | 15,600 | 16,224 | 16,873 |

Monthly bank loan repayment = (£100,000 ÷ 20) + £50 = £5,050

**63**

|  | July<br>£ | August<br>£ | September<br>£ |
|---|---|---|---|
| **RECEIPTS** |  |  |  |
| Cash sales | 1,650 | 1,950 | 2,400 |
| Credit sales | 8,325 | 9,150 | 10,250 |
| Bank loan | 12,960 | 0 | 0 |
| Interest receivable | 18 | 0 | 0 |
| **Total receipts** | 22,953 | 11,100 | 12,650 |
| **PAYMENTS** |  |  |  |
| Purchases | −7,000 | −7,210 | −7,426 |
| Wages | −4,000 | −4,000 | −4,000 |
| Expenses | −1,250 | −1,750 | −2,000 |
| Dividend payment | −15,000 | 0 | 0 |
| Bank loan repayment | 0 | −396 | −396 |
| Overdraft interest | 0 | −7 | −30 |
| **Total payments** | −27,250 | −13,363 | −13,852 |
| Net cash flow | −4,297 | −2,263 | −1,202 |
| Opening bank balance | 3,600 | −697 | −2,960 |
| **Closing bank balance** | −697 | −2,960 | −4,162 |

**Workings:**

|  | July £ | August £ | September £ |
|---|---|---|---|
| Cash sales | 11,000 × 15% = 1,650 | 13,000 × 15% = 1,950 | 16,000 × 15% = 2,400 |

|  | July £ | August £ | September £ |
|---|---|---|---|
| Credit sales: |  |  |  |
| From May | 9,000 × 40% = 3,600 |  |  |
| From June | 10,500 × 45% = 4,725 | 10,500 × 40% = 4,200 |  |
| From July |  | 11,000 × 45% = 4,950 | 11,000 × 40% = 4,400 |
| From August |  |  | 13,000 × 45% = 5,850 |
| Total credit sales receipts | 8,325 | 9,150 | 10,250 |

|  | June £ | July £ | August £ | September £ | October £ |
|---|---|---|---|---|---|
| Credit purchases | 7,000 | 7,000 × 1.03 = 7,210 | 7,210 × 1.03 = 7,426 | 7,426 × 1.03 = 7,649 | 7,649 × 1.03 = 7,879 |
| Purchase payments |  | 7,000 | 7,210 | 7,426 | 7,649 |

Monthly bank loan repayment = (£12,960 × 1.1) ÷ 36 = £396

**64**

|  | Month 3 £ | Month 4 £ |
|---|---|---|
| **RECEIPTS** |  |  |
| Sales receipts | 672,450 | 682,670 |
| Rental income |  | 2,600 |
| Investment income | 2,083 | 2,083 |
| Sale of non-current asset | 31,000 |  |
| **Total receipts** | 705,533 | 687,353 |
| **PAYMENTS** |  |  |
| Purchases | -40,150 | -50,200 |
| Wages and salaries | -94,700 | -92,100 |
| General Expenses | -6,000 | -5,000 |
| Mortgage payment | -5,583 | -5,583 |
| VAT payment to HMRC | -34,000 |  |
| Purchase of non-current assets | -£4,950 | -£4,950 |
| Overdraft interest |  |  |
| **Total payments** | -185,383 | -157,833 |
| **Net cash flow** | **520,150** | **529520** |
| Opening bank balance | 160,000 | 680,150 |
| Closing bank balance | 680,150 | 1,209,670 |

**Workings:**

|  | Month 3 £ | Month 4 £ |
|---|---|---|
| Rental income |  | £31,200 ÷ 12 = £2,600 |
| Investment income | (£500,000 × 5%) ÷ 12 = £2,083 | (£500,000 × 5%) ÷ 12 = £2,083 |
| Sale of non-current asset | (£48,000 × 50%) + £7,000 = £31,000 |  |
| Mortgage payment | (£750,000 × 80%) ÷ 15 ÷12 = £3,333<br>(£750,000 × 80%) × 0.045 ÷ 12 = £2,250<br>Total = £5,583 | (£750,000 × 80%) ÷ 15 ÷12 = £3,333<br>(£750,000 × 80%) × 0.045 ÷ 12 = £2,250<br>Total = £5,583 |
| VAT payment to HMRC | VAT on sales = £510,100 × 20% = £102,020<br>VAT on purchases = £340,100 × 20% = £68,020<br>VAT payment = £102,020 − £68,020 = £34,000 |  |
| Purchase of non-current assets | (£54,000 × 55%) ÷ 6 = -£4,950 | (£54,000 × 55%) ÷ 6 = -£4,950 |

**65**

| Cash budget | Period 5 £ | Period 6 £ |
|---|---|---|
| **Receipts** |  |  |
| Receipts from sales | 100,500 | 106,250 |
| Insurance claim |  | 125,000 × 90% × 20% = £22,500 |
| Dividend receipt | 50,000 ÷ 1.22 = £40,984 |  |
| Receipt from sale of statue | 10,000 ÷ 80 × 100 = £12,500 |  |
| **Total receipts** | 100,500 + 40,984 + 12,500 = £153,984 | 106,250 + 22,500 = £128,750 |
| **Payments** |  |  |
| Purchases | (8,510) | (9,400) |
| Payroll payments to employees | 80,300 × 88% = (£70,664) | 80,500 × 88% = (£70,840) |
| Payments to HMRC | 80,000 × 12% + 16,000 = (£25,600) | 80,300 × 12% + 16,060 = (£25,696) |
| Recruitment cost of the CEO | 7,000 + 150,000 × 20% = (£37,000) |  |
| Other expenses | (12,050) | (16,507) |
| **Total payments** | 8,510 + 70,664 + 25,600 + 37,000 + 12,050 = (£153,824) | 9,400 + 70,840 + 25,696 + 16,507 = (£122,443) |
| Net cash flow | 153,984 − 153,824 = £160 | 128,750 − 122,443 = £6,307 |
| Opening bank balance | 8,250 | £8,410 |
| **Closing bank balance** | 8,250 + 160 = £8,410 | 8,410 + 6,307 = £14,717 |

# SENSITIVITY ANALYSIS

**66** Offering prompt payment discounts to customers should **decrease** the time taken to recover debts. However, it will also **reduce** the total cash received.

**67** Taking advantage of early settlement discounts offered by suppliers will **reduce** the amount we pay overall but having to pay **earlier** may mean there is a **bigger** strain on our cash flows.

**68** (a)

| | Period 1 (£) | Period 2 (£) | Period 3 (£) | Period 4 (£) | Period 5 (£) |
|---|---|---|---|---|---|
| Original value of forecast sales | 90,000 | 95,000 | 102,500 | 94,500 | 107,500 |
| Original timing of receipts | | | 97,250 | 100,100 | 98,400 |
| Revised value of forecast sales | 72,000 | 76,000 | 82,000 | 75,600 | 86,000 |
| Revised timing of receipts | | | 75,000 | 78,960 | 79,200 |

**Workings:**

Original timing of receipts:

Period 3 = (£95,000 × 70%) + (£102,500 × 30%) = £97,250

Period 4 = (£102,500 × 70%) + (£94,500 × 30%) = £100,100

Period 5 = (£94,500 × 70%) + (£107,500 × 30%) = £98,400

Revised value of forecast receipts:

Period 1 = £90,000 × 80% = £72,000

Period 2 = £95,000 × 80% = £76,000

Period 3 = £102,500 × 80% = £82,000

Period 4 = £94,500 × 80% = £75,600

Period 5 = £107,500 × 80% = £86,000

Revised timing of receipts:

Period 3 = (£82,000 × 10%) + (£76,000 × 50%) + (£72,000 × 40%) = £75,000

Period 4 = (£75,600 × 10%) + (£82,000 × 50%) + (£76,000 × 40%) = £78,960

Period 5 = (£86,000 × 10%) + (£75,600 × 50%) + (£82,000 × 40%) = £79,200

(b)

| | Period 3 (£) | Period 4 (£) | Period 5 (£) |
|---|---|---|---|
| Original timing of payments | 22,354 | 28,601 | 21,660 |
| Revised timing of payments | 21,431 | 23,603 | 27,213 |

**Workings:**

Revised timing of payments

Period 3 = (£22,354 × 20%) + (£21,200 × 80%) = £21,431

Period 4 = (£28,601 × 20%) + (£22,354 × 80%) = £23,603

Period 5 = (£21,600 × 20%) + (£28,601 × 80%) = £27,213

(c)

|  | Period 3 (£) | Period 4 (£) | Period 5 (£) |
|---|---|---|---|
| Original net cash flow | 5,632 | 5,162 | 5,893 |
| Changes in sales receipts | –22,250 | –21,140 | –19,200 |
| Changes in purchase payments | 923 | 4,998 | –5,553 |
| Revised net cash flow | –15,695 | –10,980 | –18,860 |
| Opening bank balance | 8,597 | –7,098 | –18,078 |
| Closing bank balance | –7,098 | –18,078 | –36,938 |

**69** (a)

|  | Period 1 (£) | Period 2 (£) | Period 3 (£) | Period 4 (£) | Period 5 (£) |
|---|---|---|---|---|---|
| Original value of forecast sales | 120,000 | 135,000 | 97,500 | 133,500 | 112,500 |
| Original timing of receipts |  |  | 127,500 | 104,700 | 129,300 |
| Revised value of forecast sales | 84,000 | 94,500 | 68,250 | 93,450 | 78,750 |
| Revised timing of receipts |  |  | 87,150 | 78,540 | 85,470 |

**Workings:**

Original timing of receipts:

Period 3 = (£135,000 × 80%) + (£97,500 × 20%) = £127,500

Period 4 = (£97,500 × 80%) + (£133,500 × 20%) = £104,700

Period 5 = (£133,500 × 80%) + (£112,500 × 20%) = £129,300

Revised value of forecast receipts:

Period 1 = £120,000 × 70% = £84,000

Period 2 = £135,000 × 70% = £94,500

Period 3 = £97,500 × 70% = £68,250

Period 4 = £133,500 × 70% = £93,450

Period 5 = £112,500 × 70% = £78,750

Revised timing of receipts:

Period 3 = (£84,000 × 20%) + (£94,500 × 60%) + (£68,250 × 20%) = £87,150

Period 4 = (£94,500 × 20%) + (£68,250 × 60%) + (£93,450 × 20%) = £78,540

Period 5 = (£68,250 × 20%) + (£93,450 × 60%) + (£78,750 × 20%) = £85,470

(b)

|  | Period 3 (£) | Period 4 (£) | Period 5 (£) |
|---|---|---|---|
| Original timing of payments | 58,500 | 80,100 | 67,500 |
| Revised timing of payments (Working) | 47,250 | 50,022 | 50,778 |

**Workings:**

|  | Period 1 | Period 2 | Period 3 | Period 4 | Period 5 |
|---|---|---|---|---|---|
| Revised sales volume (70%) (items) |  | 630 | 455 | 623 | 525 |
| Revised purchases (× 90) (£) | 56,700 | 40,950 | 56,070 | 47,250 |  |
| 60% paid one month later (£) |  | 34,020 | 24,570 | 33,642 | 28,350 |
| 40% two months later (£) |  |  | 22,680 | 16,380 | 22,428 |
| Revised payments (£) |  |  | 47,250 | 50,022 | 50,778 |

(c)

|  | Period 3 (£) | Period 4 (£) | Period 5 (£) |
|---|---|---|---|
| Original net cash flow | 52,362 | 51,986 | 53,695 |
| Changes in sales receipts | −40,350 | −26,160 | −43,830 |
| Changes in purchase payments | 11,250 | 30,078 | 16,722 |
| Revised net cash flow | 23,262 | 55,904 | 26,587 |
| Opening bank balance | 18,597 | 41,859 | 97,763 |
| Closing bank balance | 41,859 | 97,763 | 124,350 |

**70** (a)

|  | Period 1 (£) | Period 2 (£) | Period 3 (£) | Period 4 (£) | Period 5 (£) |
|---|---|---|---|---|---|
| Period 1 sales | 55,860 | 28,500 | 9,500 |  |  |
| Period 2 sales |  | 61,446 | 31,350 | 10,450 |  |
| Period 3 sales |  |  | 58,653 | 29,925 | 9,975 |
| Period 4 sales |  |  |  | 89,376 | 45,600 |
| Period 5 sales |  |  |  |  | 97,755 |
| Revised forecast sales receipts | 55,860 | 89,946 | 99,503 | 129,751 | 153,330 |

**Workings:**

|  | Period 1 | Period 2 | Period 3 | Period 4 | Period 5 |
|---|---|---|---|---|---|
| Period 1 sales | 95,000 × 60% × 98% | 95,000 × 30 | 95,000 × 10% |  |  |
| Period 2 sales |  | 104,500 × 60% × 98% | 104,500 × 30% | 104,500 × 10% |  |
| Period 3 sales |  |  | 99,750 × 60% × 98% | 99,750 × 30% | 99,750 × 10% |
| Period 4 sales |  |  |  | 152,000 × 60% × 98% | 152,000 × 30% |
| Period 5 sales |  |  |  |  | 166,250 × 60% × 98% |

(b) Total receipts from sales in periods 1 to 3 **increase** by **6.9%** if the settlement discount is offered.

**Workings:**

Original receipts in periods 1 to 3 = £28,500 + £97,850 + £103,075 = £229,425

Revised receipts in periods 1 to 3 = £55,860 + £89,946 + £99,503 = £245,309

Difference = £245,309 − £229,425 = £15,884

Difference as a percentage of original = £15,884 ÷ 229,425 × 100 = 6.9%

**71** (a)

|  | Period 1 (£) | Period 2 (£) | Period 3 (£) | Period 4 (£) | Period 5 (£) |
|---|---|---|---|---|---|
| Original value of forecast sales | 32,400 | 34,200 | 36,900 | 34,020 | 38,700 |
| Revised value of forecast sales | 23,400 | 34,200 | 32,400 | 34,020 | 38,700 |
| Original timing of receipts |  |  | 34,425 | 34,812 | 36,810 |
| Revised timing of receipts |  |  | 29,250 | 33,687 | 35,010 |

**Workings:**

Revised value of forecast sales:

Period 1 = £32,400 − (500 × £18) = £23,400

Period 3 = £36,900 − (250 × £18) = £32,400

Revised timing of receipts:

Period 3 = (£32,400 × 35%) + (£34,200 × 25%) + (£23,400 × 40%) = £29,250

Period 4 = (£34,020 × 35%) + (£32,400 × 25%) + (£34,200 × 40%) = £33,687

Period 5 = (£38,700 × 35%) + (£34,020 × 25%) + (£32,400 × 40%) = £35,010

(b)

|  | Period 3 (£) | Period 4 (£) | Period 5 (£) |
|---|---|---|---|
| Payments for purchases | 18,650 | 18,315 | 19,810 |

**Workings:**

|  | Period 1 | Period 2 | Period 3 | Period 4 | Period 5 |
|---|---|---|---|---|---|
| Sales volume | 1,300 | 1,900 | 1,800 | 1,890 | 2,150 |
| Purchases £ | 19,000 | 18,000 | 18,900 | 21,500 |  |
| Payments |  |  |  |  |  |
| From Period 1 |  | 19,000 × 35% | 19,000 × 65% |  |  |
| From Period 2 |  |  | 18,000 × 35% | 18,000 × 65% |  |
| From Period 3 |  |  |  | 18,900 × 35% | 18,900 × 65% |
| From Period 4 |  |  |  |  | 21,500 × 35% |
| Total payments |  |  | 18,650 | 18,315 | 19,810 |

(c)

|  | (£) |
|---|---|
| Opening bank balance period 3 | 3,200 |
| Total sales receipts | 97,947 |
| Total purchase payments | −56,775 |
| Closing bank balance period 5 | 44,372 |

**72** (a)

|  | Period 1 (£) | Period 2 (£) | Period 3 (£) | Period 4 (£) | Period 5 (£) |
|---|---|---|---|---|---|
| Revised value of forecast sales | 26,307 | 26,919 | 28,515 | 27,651 | 29,366 |
| Revised timing of receipts |  |  | 26,883 | 27,667 | 28,297 |

**Workings:**

|  | Period 1 | Period 2 | Period 3 | Period 4 | Period 5 |
|---|---|---|---|---|---|
| Sales value (£) | 30,100 | 30,800 | 32,620 | 31,640 | 33,600 |
| Sales volume (value ÷ £14) | 2,150 | 2,200 | 2,330 | 2,260 | 2,400 |
| Revised sales volume (92%) | 1,978 | 2,024 | 2,144 | 2,079 | 2,208 |
| Revised sales value (£13.30) | 26,307 | 26,919 | 28,515 | 27,651 | 29,366 |
| Revised timing of receipts |  |  |  |  |  |
| From Period 1 | 26,307 × 15% | 26,307 × 40% | 26,307 × 45% |  |  |
| From Period 2 |  | 26,919 × 15% | 26,919 × 40% | 26,919 × 45% |  |
| From Period 3 |  |  | 28,515 × 15% | 28,515 × 40% | 28,515 × 45% |
| From Period 4 |  |  |  | 27,651 × 15% | 27,651 × 40% |
| From Period 5 |  |  |  |  | 29,366 × 15% |
| Total receipts |  |  | 26,883 | 27,667 | 28,297 |

(b)

|  | Period 3 (£) | Period 4 (£) | Period 5 (£) |
|---|---|---|---|
| Revised timing of payments | 7,500 | 8,493 | 9,656 |

**Workings:**

|  | Period 3 (£) | Period 4 (£) | Period 5 (£) |
|---|---|---|---|
| From Period 1 | 8,580 × 30% |  |  |
| From Period 2 | 7,600 × 30% | 7,600 × 30% |  |
| From Period 3 | 6,820 × 40% × 97% | 6,820 × 30% | 6,820 × 30% |
| From Period 4 |  | 10,740 × 40% × 97% | 10,740 × 30% |
| From Period 5 |  |  | 11,310 × 40% × 97% |
| Total payments | 7,500 | 8,493 | 9,656 |

(c)

|  | Period 3 (£) | Period 4 (£) | Period 5 (£) |
|---|---|---|---|
| Original net cash flow | 276 | 153 | 219 |
| Changes in sales receipts | −4,827 | −4,463 | −4,323 |
| Changes in purchase payments | 100 | −1,673 | 1,084 |
| Revised net cash flow | −4,451 | −5,983 | −3,020 |
| Opening bank balance | 790 | −3,661 | −9,644 |
| Closing bank balance | −3,661 | −9,644 | −12,664 |

**73** (a)

|  | Period 1 (£) | Period 2 (£) | Period 3 (£) |
|---|---|---|---|
| Payments |  |  |  |
| Purchases | 14,400 | 16,800 | 18,144 |
| Other production expenses | 6,420 | 6,634 | 7,169 |
| Wages and salaries | 8,250 | 9,020 | 9,225 |
| Rent | 12,000 | 12,400 | 12,400 |
| Total payments | 41,070 | 44,854 | 46,938 |

**Workings:**

|  | Period 1 (£) | Period 2 (£) | Period 3 (£) |
|---|---|---|---|
| Payments |  |  |  |
| Purchases | 15,000 × 96% | 17,500 × 96% | 18,900 × 96% |
| Other production expenses | 6,000 × 1.07 | 6,200 × 1.07 | 6,700 × 1.07 |
| Wages and salaries | 8,250 | 8,800 × 1.025 | 9,000 × 1.025 |
| Rent | 12,000 | 12,000 + 400 | 12,000 + 400 |

(b) The effect of the changes to payments is to **increase** the quarterly cash outflow by **£712**.

**Workings:**

Original total payments = £41,250 + £44,400 + £46,500 = £132,150

Revised total payments = £41,070 + £44,854 + £46,938 = £132,862

Difference = £132,862 − £132,150 = £712

**74** (a)

|  | January (£) | February (£) | March (£) | Total (£) |
|---|---|---|---|---|
| Sales receipts | 29,040 | 23,232 | 33,880 | 86,152 |
| Payments |  |  |  |  |
| Material | 6,600 | 5,280 | 7,700 | 19,580 |
| Labour | 4,620 | 3,696 | 5,390 | 13,706 |
| Overheads | 6,960 | 6,168 | 7,620 | 20,748 |

**Workings:**

|  | January | February | March |
|---|---|---|---|
| Sales receipts | 30,000 × 1.1 × 0.88 | 24,000 × 1.1 × 0.88 | 35,000 × 1.1 × 0.88 |
| Payments |  |  |  |
| Revised production | 30,000 ÷ £20 × 0.88 = 1,320 | 24,000 ÷ £20 × 0.88 = 1,056 | 35,000 ÷ £20 × 0.88 = 1,540 |
| Material | 1,320 × £5 | 1,056 × £5 | 1,540 × £5 |
| Labour | 1,320 × 0.25 × £14 | 1,056 × 0.25 × £14 | 1,540 × 0.25 × £14 |
| Overheads | £3,000 + (1,320 × £3) | £3,000 + (1,056 × £3) | £3,000 + (1,540 × £3) |

(b)

|  | £ |
|---|---|
| Original closing cash balance at 31 March | 32,450 |
| Change in sales receipts | −2,848 |
| Change in material cost | 2,670 |
| Change in labour cost | 12,994 |
| Change in overhead cost | 1,602 |
| Revised closing cash balance at 31 March | 46,868 |

**Workings:**

Original closing balance at 31st March = £14,750 + £89,000 − £71,300 = £32,450

**75**

| Period | 1 (£) | 2 (£) | 3 (£) |
|---|---|---|---|
| New machinery | −750,000 | −750,000 | 0 |
| *Increase in sales* | 500,000 | 500,000 | 500,000 |
| Receipt of cash | 250,000 | 500,000 | 500,000 |
| Net cash flow | −500,000 | −250,000 | 500,000 |

The cumulative cash flow for periods 1 – 3 will **decrease** by £250,000

**76**  Increase in hours worked = 50 employees × 37 hours × 4 weeks × 25% = 1,850 hours

Overtime payment = 1,850 hours × £10.50 = £19,425

Increase in cash receipts = £25,000

The cumulative cash flow for the next four weeks will **increase** by £5,575

**77**  (a)

| Month | January £ | February £ | March £ | April £ |
|---|---|---|---|---|
| Revised purchases | 230,000 + 290,000 + 230,000 + 270,000 = 1,025,000<br><br>1,020,000 ÷ 4 = £255,000 | £255,000 | £255,000 | £255,000 |

| Forecast purchase payments | 255,000 × 98% × 50% = £124,950 | 255,000 × 98% × 50% = £124,950 | 255,000 × 98% × 50% = £124,950 | 255,000 × 98% × 50% = £124,950 |
| | | 255,000 × 10% = £25,500 | 255,000 × 50% = £127,500 | 255,000 × 50% = £127,500 |
| | | Total £150,450 | Total £252,450 | Total £252,450 |

(b)    £255,000 × 50% × 2% × 4 = **£10,200**

# MONITORING CASH BUDGETS

**78**    (a)

| | Variance £ | Adverse/ Favourable |
|---|---|---|
| Budgeted closing bank balance | 3,198 | |
| Shortfall in receipts from receivables | 6,820 | A |
| Increase in cash sales | 954 | F |
| Decrease in payments to payables | 11,566 | F |
| Increase in cash purchases | 200 | A |
| Increase in capital expenditure | 24,500 | A |
| Decrease in wages and salaries | 2,090 | F |
| Decrease in general expenses | 1,500 | F |
| Actual closing bank balance | (12,212) | |

(b)    **C**

Delayed capital expenditure

**Note:** Although the other options could have resulted in a lower overdraft they are not sufficient in themselves to reduce the deficit by £12,212

(c)

| | |
|---|---|
| Rates of income tax have increased labour costs | Reduce hours worked |
| Customers are buying lower value products | Actively market more expensive product lines |
| Suppliers are insisting on earlier payments | Negotiate early settlement discount |
| Customers are taking more days to settle their debts | Improve credit control |
| Prices of raw materials have increased | Change suppliers |

**79**

| Variance | (a) Could be caused by: | (b) Corrective action: |
|---|---|---|
| Shortfall in receipts | Customers are taking more time to settle their debts.<br>Decrease in sales volume/value.<br>Inaccurate forecasting.<br>Economic/environmental factors affecting sales. | Improve credit control.<br>Improve product.<br>Increase marketing/advertising.<br>Revise future budgets. |
| Shortfall in cash sales | Fewer cash sales.<br>More customers taking credit. | As above and also check that strict controls are being followed when offering credit. |
| Increase in payments to payables | Buying better quality raw material. | Check to see if better quality material is improving product.<br>Arrange better payment terms. |
| Increase in cash purchases | Obtained discounts by buying more for cash.<br>Some suppliers not offering credit terms. | Adjust future forecasts for cash payments.<br>Investigate why credit terms not being offered. |
| Increase in capital expenditure | Earlier expenditure has been deferred.<br>Unexpected expenditure incurred. | Better forecasting. |
| Decrease in wages and salaries | Training has reduced hours worked.<br>Sales volumes declining so manufacturing is decreasing.<br>Less overtime than budgeted.<br>Reduction in staff numbers. | Adjust future budgets to reflect the improvements if due to efficiencies. |

**80**

| | Budgeted (£) | Actual (£) | Variance (£) | A/F |
|---|---|---|---|---|
| RECEIPTS | | | | |
| Cash sales | 4,200 | 3,800 | 400 | A |
| Credit sales | 42,100 | 48,000 | 5,900 | F |
| Total receipts | 46,300 | 51,800 | 5,500 | F |
| | | | | |
| PAYMENTS | | | | |
| Cash purchases | 500 | −1,200 | 700 | A |
| Credit purchases | 28,000 | −35,100 | 7,100 | A |
| Labour costs | 2,500 | −3,200 | 700 | A |
| Capital expenditure | 8,000 | −6,000 | 2,000 | F |
| General expenses | 4,000 | −3,800 | 200 | F |
| Total payments | 43,000 | −49,300 | 6,300 | A |
| | | | | |
| Net cash flow | 3,300 | 2,500 | 800 | A |

**81**  (a)

| | £ | Adverse or Favourable |
|---|---|---|
| Budgeted closing bank balance | 6,455 | |
| Receipts from receivables | 4,756 | A |
| Cash sales | 570 | A |
| Payments to payables | 2,173 | A |
| Cash payments | 940 | A |
| Capital expenditure | 12,000 | A |
| Wages and salaries | 3,600 | F |
| General expenses | 4,136 | F |
| Actual closing bank balance | (6,248) | |

(b)   Shortfall in receipts and cash sales – improve credit control, improve the product, increase advertising and marketing.

Increase in cash and credit payments – arrange better credit terms with suppliers, investigate other suppliers or materials that may be cheaper.

Capital expenditure could be delayed or another form of finance could be used.

**82**   **Sales (6% adverse)**

*Possible reasons*

- Delays in collection of cash from receivables
- Decrease in production volume therefore sales volume due to the machine breaking down
- Reduction in selling price in line with competition
- Inaccurate forecasting

*Possible actions*

- Improve credit control/tighten up credit terms
- Consider keeping more inventory of the product in case of emergencies (machine breaking down)
- Improvement to the product to increase sales
- Better advertising of product
- Reflect any price changes in future budgets if they are to be maintained

**Investment income (18% adverse)**

*Possible reasons*

- Drop in bank base rate which has affected the rate of interest of the investment
- Inaccurate forecasting

*Possible actions*

- Research other investments for a better more stable return – possibly look for a fixed interest investment
- Amend future budgets to reflect the change in interest rate.

**Labour cost (9% favourable)**

*Possible reasons*

- If production volume has dropped due to the machine breakdown direct wages may fall
- Less overtime being worked
- Reduction in staff numbers

*Possible actions*

- Future budgets may need to be adjusted if a reduction in manufacturing/staff numbers is to be maintained.
- If efficiencies have improved in the work force this should be reflected in future budgets.

**Capital expenditure (28% adverse)**

*Possible reasons*

- Replacement of broken machine
- Deferral of earlier planned expenditure
- Unexpected expenditure
- Price increase since budget
- Higher specification of assets purchased

*Possible actions*

- Better planning in the future
- Use of other forms of finance to fund purchases (leasing, hire purchase, loan)
- Deferral to a later period

# LIQUIDITY MANAGEMENT

## WORKING CAPITAL CYCLE/CASH OPERATING CYCLE

**83** **C**

**84** **D**

**85** 80 + 40 − 45 = 75 so correct choice is **C**

**86** The cash operating cycle will decrease by 2 days – the increase in inventory holding days increases the length of the cycle, the increase in the payment period decreases the length of the cycle – the net effect is a decrease of 2 days.

**87** The cash operating cycle will increase by 7 days – the increase in the receivables period increases the length of the cycle, the decrease in inventory holding days decreases the length of the cycle – the net effect is an increase of 7 days.

**88** The answer is 44.24 days.

**Receivables**

|  | £ |  | £ |
|---|---|---|---|
| B/f | 68,000 | Returns | 2,500 |
| Sales | 250,000 | Cash | 252,100 |
|  |  | Irrecoverable debts |  |
|  |  | (68,000 × 0.05) | 3,400 |
|  |  | C/f | 60,000 |
|  | _____ |  | _____ |
|  | 318,000 |  | 318,000 |
|  | _____ |  | _____ |

Receivable days = 60/247.5 × (365/2) = 44.24 days

**89** **B**

|  | £ |
|---|---|
| Balance b/fwd | 22,000 |
| Credit sales | 290,510 |
|  | 312,510 |
| Less: Balance c/fwd (£290,510 × 49/365) | (39,000) |
| Receipts | 273,510 |

**90    60.8 days**

|  |  | Days |
|---|---|---|
| Inventory | (0.8/3) × 365 | 97.3 |
| Trade receivables | (0.4/4) × 365 | 36.5 |
| Trade payables | (0.3/1.5) × 365 | (73.0) |
| Cash operating cycle |  | 60.8 |

**91**    (a)

|  | Working | 31 May 20X5 |
|---|---|---|
| Sales revenue | Receivable days = Rec ÷ Rev × 365<br>44.1 = 290,000 ÷ Rev × 365<br>Rev = 290,000 ÷ 44.1 × 365 | 2,400,000 |
| Cost of sales | 2,400,000 – 1,000,000 | 1,400,000 |
| Inventories level in the statement of financial position | Inventory days = Inv ÷ COS × 365<br>93.9 = Inv ÷ 1,400,000 × 365<br>Inv = 93.9 ÷ 365 × 1,400,000 | 360,000 |
| Trade payables payment period in days (1 decimal place) | 190,000 ÷ 1,400,000 × 365 | 49.6 |

(b)    The cash operating cycle for DX is 44.1 + 93.9 – 49.6 = 88.4 days

**92**

| | | | |
|---|---|---|---|
| (i) | Inventory days | 220/1800 × 365 | 44.6 |
| (ii) | Receivables days | 350/(0.85 × 2,600) × 365 | 57.8 |
| (iii) | Payables days | 260/(0.90 × 1,650) × 365 | 63.9 |

**93**    (b)    The inventory holding period is 150 ÷ 1,300 × 365 = 42 days

The trade receivables collection period is 300 ÷ 2,700 × 365 = 41 days

The trade payable payment period is 230 ÷ 1,300 × 365 = 65 days

(c)    The cash operating cycle is 42 + 41 – 65 = 18 days

**94    C**

Average receivables = (£10 million + £12 million)/2 = £11 million

Average trade-related receivables = 90% × £11 million = £9.9 million

Annual sales on credit = £95 million

Average collection period = (£9.9 million/£95 million) × 365 days = 38 days

**95**    To improve the working capital cycle, a business could **decrease** its debt collection period and/or **extend** the credit period it obtains from its suppliers.

**96** The answer is £4,800.

| | Current assets | Current liabilities |
|---|---|---|
| | £ | £ |
| Credit purchase: | | |
| Inventory | + 18,000 | |
| Trade payables | | + 18,000 |
| Credit sale: | | |
| Trade receivables | + 24,000 | |
| Inventory (24,000 × 100/125) | − 19,200 | |

Working capital will increase by £4,800, as a result of the credit sale.

**97** The answer is £6.75m

Cos = £30m × 70% = £21m

Inventory months = Inventory value/CoS × 12

2.5 = Inv/21 × 12

2.5/12 × 21 = 4.375

Receivable months = Receivables/Revenue × 12

2.0 = Receivables/30 × 12

2.0/12 × 30 = 5

Payable months = Payables/CoS × 12

1.5 = Pay/21 × 12

1.5/12 × 21 = 2.625

Working capital = £4.375 + £5 − £2.625 = £6.75m

**98** Over capitalisation is a situation where a firm has **more** working capital than it needs.

**99** (i) Overtrading means a company it growing too quickly without the long term finance to support its growth. This will result in rapid increase in turnover, high levels of inventory, receivables, payables, little increase in share capital and long term loans and problems with liquidity when short term funding is used to support the growth.

(ii) The actions HL could take to correct the problem could be:

- Inject more long term capital into the business by issuing more share capital or raising long term loans
- Cut back on trading and be more selective of who they sell to
- Reduce the working capital cycle to improve liquidity, i.e. chase receivables to collect cash faster, reduce inventory levels and delay payables within reason.

## GOVERNMENT MONETARY POLICY

**100 B**

Quantitative easing is not normally considered, as it would rapidly increase the money supply, resulting in high inflation. Instead, other measures, such as reducing interest rates could be considered. However, during the ongoing financial crisis, many countries already have very low interest rates and the threat of high inflation is not considered significant compared to the need to boost liquidity in the banking system and hence the economy.

**101** Central banks try to increase the amount of lending and activity in the economy indirectly, by lowering interest rates. Lower interest rates encourage people to spend, not save.

**102** (i)   Fiscal policy

   (ii)   Monetary policy

**103 B**

**104 B**

**105 D**

**106**

| Statement | True | False |
|---|---|---|
| The Bribery Act covers all aspects of white collar crime | | ✓ |
| Money laundering regulations cover only accountants | | ✓ |

## INTEREST RATES

**107 A**

**108 B**

**109 D**

**110 B**

**111** The term used to describe the effective rate of interest that a borrower will pay on a loan.

# RAISING FINANCE

**112  E**

**113  C**

**114**  Total repayments = £5,500 × 12 = £66,000

Interest paid = £66,000 − £60,000 = £6,000

Interest rate = £6,000 ÷ £60,000 × 100 = 10%

**115**  Total repayments = £4,000 × 12 × 5 = £240,000

Interest paid = £240,000 - £200,000 = £40,000

Interest rate = £40,000 ÷ £200,000 × 100 ÷ 5 years = 4%

**116**  100,000 × 2% = £2,000 interest pa

£2,000 × 3 = £6,000

(£100,000 + £6,000) ÷ 36 = £2,944

**117**

|  | Month 3 | Month 4 | Month 5 | Month 6 | Month 7 |
|---|---|---|---|---|---|
| Forecast net cash flow | 7,500 | -7,500 | 15,000 | -15,000 | -10,000 |
| Opening balance | -5,000 | 2,500 | -5,062.50 | 9,937.50 | -5,125.78 |
| Closing balance before interest | 2,500 | -5,000 | 9,937.50 | -5,062.50 | -15,125.78 |
| Overdraft interest to be charged | 0 | -62.5 | 0 | -63.28 | -189.07 |

**118**  12/250 × 100 = 4.8%

**119  A**

**120**

| Statement | True | False |
|---|---|---|
| A floating charge is security on a loan supplied by a group of assets | ✓ | |
| A fixed charge is security on a loan supplied by a specific asset | ✓ | |

**121  A**

**122** A bank facility letter sets out the **legal** rights and duties of **the bank and the customer** when the bank grants an **overdraft and or a loan**.

The purpose of a facility letter is to protect the rights **the bank and the customer**.

A bank loan is often **less** expensive than an overdraft, mainly due to the **lower** interest rates.

An overdraft can be **cheaper** overall because we only borrow what's needed, on a daily basis.

**123**

|  |  | Loan interest £ | Capital repayments £ | Arrangement fee £ | Overdraft interest £ | Total cost £ |
|---|---|---|---|---|---|---|
| Option 1 | Year 1 | 6,000 | 25,000 | 1,500 | 2,400 |  |
|  | Year 2 | 4,000 | 25,000 | – | – |  |
|  |  | 10,000 | 50,000 | 1,500 | 2,400 | 63,900 |
| Option 2 | Year 1 | 6,660 | 37,000 | 1,110 | – |  |
|  | Year 2 | 4,440 | 37,000 | – | – |  |
|  |  | 11,100 | 74,000 | 1,110 | – | 86,210 |

**Option 1**

Option 2 has the higher total cost over the two years considered.

**124** Currently the company is incurring two costs that could be saved if they accepted the without recourse facility offered by Cashrich Credit plc.

**Savings**

| | |
|---|---|
| Admin costs of sales ledger | £15,000 |
| Interest – 8% of £500,000 × 85% | £34,000 |
| Total savings | £49,000 |

**Costs**

| | |
|---|---|
| Charges £3,000,000 × 2½% | £75,000 |

As the costs exceed the savings, it would not be in the company's interest to accept the facility.

**125**

| Statement | True | False |
|---|---|---|
| Invoice discounting passes control of the sales ledger and credit control function to the invoice discounting company |  | ✓ |

**126   Hire purchase agreement**

- A hire purchase agreement will enable the company to purchase the plant and pay for it in instalments over 5 years.

- Interest will be charged based on the balance outstanding and an interest rate set at the beginning of the finance term.

- The plant will remain the property of the hire purchase company until all the instalments have been made however the company will be responsible for repairs and maintenance during the term of the hire purchase agreement.

- As the company will have substantially all of the risks and rewards of ownership the plant will be shown on the statement of financial position as an asset at its full purchase price.

- The balance of the hire purchase outstanding will be shown as a liability on the statement of financial position. The amount due within one year will be included with current liabilities and the balance with non-current liabilities.

- Interest paid on the loan will be debited to the statement of profit or loss.

- The balance of the loan in non-current liabilities is classed as long term debt and will therefore be included in the gearing calculation.

- The gearing of the company will increase which could affect the company's ability to raise additional finance. The plant will not be available for other lenders to take as security because the hire purchase company will hold title until the final repayment has been made.

**Operating lease**

- An operating lease is where the risk and reward is substantially retained by the leasing company (lessor) and the lessee is effectively renting the asset.

- This is a straight forward lease agreement where the company would hire or rent the plant.

- The lessor would retain ownership of the assets.

- An operating lease is not recognised on the statement of financial position, but has to be shown in a note detailing the annual commitments which cannot be cancelled. An operating lease is 'off balance sheet'.

- The lease/rental payments are included in the statement of profit or loss as an expense.

- The payments will be spread over the term of the lease so cash outflows will be spread over 6 years for a 6 year lease.

- The company will show reduced profits due to the lease repayments.

- The gearing of the company will be unaffected as the lease is 'off balance sheet'.

- Therefore the total debt on the statement of financial position will be unaffected by the lease and the asset value is also unaffected, but a competent credit risk analyst will consider the size of the lease commitment and estimate a revised gearing position based upon including the operating lease as finance.

**Equity injection**

- The company will raise funds from the existing shareholders of the business, from new shareholders or from a combination of both.

- The additional funds raised will be used to purchase the plant outright.

- The plant will be included in non-current assets on the statement of financial position.

- There will not be any cost from this method of raising finance to the statement of profit or loss because there will be no borrowing associated with the asset and therefore no interest payments to be made.

- The equity position on the statement of financial position will increase which will have the effect of reducing gearing assuming that there is no increase in long term borrowings.

- The company will be in a stronger position to raise additional finance with lower gearing and the plant available as security.

- If the shares are offered to new investors then existing shareholders will experience a dilution of control and possibly earnings which may cause discontent.

**Taking out a bank loan**

- A bank loan is a contractual agreement for a specific sum, loaned for a fixed period, at an agreed rate of interest.

- The term of a loan should not exceed the life of the asset being purchased and will normally be approximately the same as the asset's useful life.

- The interest on the loan will either be fixed or variable. If the interest is variable then the interest charged will depend upon market rates of interest. If the interest on the loan is fixed rate then this is often more expensive than an overdraft or a variable rate loan. You will end up paying more for the asset than it would have cost for cash.

- The bank may only be prepared to advance the money on the basis of some security given by the business. Security can be in the form of a fixed charge or a floating charge. The bank would have the right to sell this asset if the business defaults on the loan repayments.

- The bank may impose certain restrictions or covenants which will limit the freedom of action of the management of the business, for example restrictions on payment of dividends or on other forms of finance taken out by the business.

- The loan will sit as a long term liability on the statement of financial position.

- The interest and repayment charges will be put through the statement of profit or loss.

- Gearing will be increased as there is an increase in debt finance.

**Funding using bonds**

- Also known as loan stock or debentures. The bond is recorded as a non-current liability on the statement of financial position and any interest to be paid will be recorded on the statement of profit or loss in the finance cost.

- Loan stock commonly has a fixed rate of interest, although in recent years a number of companies have issued floating rate debentures. They are repaid at a specified date.

- Cheaper than equity.

- Defers repayment until end of life of loan.

- It is generally cheaper to raise than a new issue of equity.

- It may be cheaper to finance than equity since debenture-holders suffer less risk and may be satisfied by a lower return. However, the gearing of the company will increase so shareholders may perceive there to be a greater risk if the company is already highly financed and may therefore require a higher return. Any future financing may be affected, as future lenders will consider the level of debt already in existence.

- The existing shareholders will retain the same degree of control.

- The company may be committed to the fixed interest payments and will therefore have less flexibility than with equity.

- In the event of any default on the interest payments, the debenture-holders would have the power to appoint a receiver to run the company.

**Debt factoring**

- Factoring is the sale of debts to a third party (the factor) at a discount in return for prompt cash. The debts of the company are effectively sold to a factor (normally owned by a bank). The factor takes on the responsibility of collecting the debt for a fee.

- A factor can save the company the administration costs of keeping the sales ledger up to date and the costs of debt collection.

- Non-recourse factoring is a convenient way of obtaining insurance against irrecoverable debts.

- Although factors provide valuable services, companies are sometimes wary about using them. A possible problem with factoring is that the intervention of the factor between the factor's client and the receivable could endanger trading relationships and damage goodwill. Customers might prefer to deal with the business, not a factor.

- When a nonrecourse factoring service is used, the client loses control over decisions about granting credit to its customers.

- There is no impact on the gearing of the company and very little impact on the financial statements.

**127** The key difference is who has access to the 'risk and reward' of the asset.

**Operating lease**

- The risks and rewards of the asset are not transferred to the lessee.

- Lease payments are an expense in the Statement of Profit or Loss, rather like rental payments.

- The asset is not included within non-current assets on the Statement of Financial Position.

- The lessor maintains the asset.

- The gearing of the company will be unaffected as the lease is 'off balance sheet'.

- The total debt on the statement of financial position will be unaffected by the lease and the asset value is also unaffected, but a competent credit risk analyst will consider the size of the lease commitment and estimate a revised gearing position based upon including the operating lease as finance.

**Finance lease**

- All the risks and rewards are transferred to the lessee.

- The lessee will be responsible for the upkeep and maintenance of the asset and to all intents and purposes owns the asset. The finance lease charges will reflect the repayment of the value of the asset and the finance charge to the lessor.

- A finance lease has to be shown on the statement of financial position by capitalising the asset and including the loan element of the lease as borrowing.

- The finance lease includes implicit interest charges which will be charged as an expense in the statement of profit or loss.

- The cash balance will not be affected by the acquisition but will be reduced by the lease payments.

- The payments will be spread over the term of the lease, aiding short term cash flow.

- The gearing of the company will increase because the asset base increases but so does the total debt.
- The increase in gearing could affect the company's ability to raise additional finance.
- The net assets will be unchanged at acquisition but the debt will increase.
- The statement of profit or loss will recognise the interest element of the finance lease payments but not the capital repayment element.
- However, the asset will be depreciated over the lease term, or perhaps longer if the useful economic life is greater. Therefore a depreciation charge will go to statement of profit or loss.

**128    Option 1**

£2,500 + (60 × £800) + £2,000 = £52,500

A payment of £2,500 extra

A percentage of £2,500/£50,000 × 100 = 5%

**Option 2**

£2,500 + (30 × £1,750) = £55,000

A payment of £5,000 extra

A percentage of £5,000/£50,000 × 100 = 10%

Based on interest rate and overall cost – **option 1** should be chosen.

**129    Option 1**

Set up cost = £1,500,000 × 2% = £30,000

Total interest = £1,500,000 × 8% ÷ 12 × 18 = £180,000

Total cost of loan = £1,500,000 + £180,000 + £30,000 = £1,710,000

Monthly repayments = (£1,500,000 + £180,000) ÷ 18 = £93,333

First month's payment = £93,333 + £30,000 = £123,333

**Option 2**

The company will be paying the £91,836 in the final month to own the asset so the cost that needs to be spread over 17 months = £1,500,000 + £152,793 - £91,836 = £1,560,957

Monthly repayments = £1,560,957 ÷ 17 = £91,821

Total cost of hire purchase = (£91,821 × 17) + £91,836 = £1,652,793

Which can also be calculated as £1,500,000 + £152,793 = £1,652,793

**Option 3**

The length of the lease term is not provided so for a comparison of costs:

Repayment over 18 months of £104,166 × 18 months = £1,874,988

**130**

    **(a)**    **How much interest and administration charge will be paid is option 1 is taken?**

        Total repayments = £4,444 × 90 = £399,960

        Interest = £399,960 - £300,000 = £99,960

        Interest and administration charge = £99,960 + £1,500 = £101,460

    **(b)**    **How much interest and administration charge will be paid if option 2 is taken?**

        Annual interest = £300,000 × 5% = £15,000

        Interest over life of the loan = £15,000 × 7.5 years = £112,500

        Interest and administration charge = £112,500 + £1,000 = £113,500

    **(c)**    **How much is the quarterly repayment for option 2?**

        Quarterly interest = £15,000 ÷ 4 = £3,750

        Quarterly capital repayment = £300,000 ÷ 30 = £10,000

        Total repayment = £3,750 + £10,000 = £13,750

    **(d)**    **How much interest and administration fee will be paid if option 3 is taken?**

        Total interest = £150,000 × 11% × 7 = £115,500

        Total administration = £800 × 7 = £5,600

        Total interest and administration = £115,500 + £5,600 = £121,100

**131**

    **(a)**    **Complete the accounting entry which would have been made on the day the loan was received.**

| Account | Debit | Credit | Amount £ |
|---|---|---|---|
| Current bank account | ✓ | | 1,500,000 |
| Current loan account | | ✓ | 1,500,000 ÷ 6 = £250,000 |
| Long-term loan account | | ✓ | £1,500,000 - £250,000 = £1,250,000 |

**(b)** Complete the missing figures. Round your answer to the nearest £000

| Extract of the Trial balance | 31st March 20X7 | 31st March 20X6 |
|---|---|---|
| Plant and machinery | 8,000 | 6,300 |
| Inventories | 3,000 | 2,500 |
| Trade receivables | 2,100 | 2,100 |
| Bank current account | 60 | (60) |
| Trade payable | (5,700) | (5,100) |
| Other creditors | (1,900) | (1,600) |
| Current portion of long term loan | (250) | (250) |
| Long term loan | Full years repayment of £250,000<br><br>Amount outstanding = £1,125,000 − £250,000 = £875,000<br><br>(£875) | 6 months repayment = 250,000 ÷ 2 = 125,000<br><br>Amount outstanding = £1,250,000 - £125,000 = £1,125,000<br><br>(£1,125) |
| Retained profit | (4,900) | (3,300) |
| Share capital | (500) | (500) |
| | | |
| Turnover | (59,700) | (57,600) |
| Purchases | 43,600 | 42,700 |
| Other operating costs | 13,300 | 12,600 |
| Long term loan interest | 68 | 40 |
| Taxation | 1,200 | 1,200 |

**(c)** Calculate the gearing for both years. Round your answer to the nearest whole percent.

| | 20X7 | 20X6 |
|---|---|---|
| Gearing | (250+875)/(250+875+4900+500) × 100 = 17.24% = **17%** | (60+250+1125)/(60+250+1125+3300+500) × 100 = 27.41% = **27%** |

**132**

**Option 1: Bank Loan**

Cost of Loan

Total interest £1,000,000 x 6% × 2 = £120,000

Setup cost £120,000 x 12.5% = £15,000

Total cost of loan = £135,000

Monthly repayment if arrangement fee is spread over life of the loan = £1,135,000/24 = £47,292

First month if arrangement fee is not spread = (£1,120,000 ÷ 24) + £15,000 = £61,667, then monthly payments of £46,667

Advantages of Loan

- Generally loans can be tailored to suit the business e.g. period, repayment schedule and interest rates
- Generally lower interest rates than other finance options
- The repayments are fixed so good for budgeting purposes
- Payment holidays may be allowed

Disadvantages of Loan

- Interest charged on the initial loan balance so no account taken of payments made.
- Penalties for early repayment
- Security may be needed
- Covenants may be needed
- Charge may be placed on asset or asset(s)

Accounting Treatment

- The setup fee and interest for year 1 will be charged to the statement of profit or loss in year 1 and the interest for year 2 will be charged to the statement of profit or loss in year 2.
- The credit rating may suffer
- The balance of the loan will be split between current liabilities and non-current liabilities in the statement of financial position.
- Only the current liability amount will have a bearing on the liquidity ratio.
- The total amount of the balance outstanding on the loan will be included in the gearing calculation.
- The gearing of the company will increase which could affect the company's ability to raise additional finance.

**Option 2 Debt Factoring**

Costs of Debt Factoring

Will increase non-current asset levels by £1m in the statement of financial position.

Initial cost to the company £250,000 (25% 0.25/1.0)

Invoice (debt) factoring is a way of raising finance quickly by selling your trade receivables/unpaid invoices to a debt factoring company.

The factor will pay the company to take on your outstanding invoices.

Typically they would pay 85% of the invoice values immediately.

The factor manages the sales ledger and chasing of the payment.

Suppliers are aware the credit control has been outsourced.

There are two types namely recourse and non-recourse. Recourse factoring is where the company retains the risk of bad debts. Recourse factoring is cheaper. Non-recourse factoring is where the factor takes on the risk of bad debts. Non-recourse factoring is more expensive

Advantages of Invoice Factoring

- Obtain cash quickly
- Secures more cash than an overdraft based on outstanding invoices (usually 50%)
- Reduces time and cost spend on credit control/debt collection

Disadvantages of Invoice Factoring

- Fee charged for factoring
- Factor takes over sales ledger
- Damage to customer relationships
- Alerts customers that there may be cash flow problems in the business
- Factor may impose constraints on the way you do business
- Ending a factoring arrangement could be difficult

Accounting Treatment

- Factoring fees will be recorded as an expense in the statement of profit or loss.
- With non-recourse factoring any debts not collected will be borne by the factor.
- With recourse factoring any irrecoverable debts will be borne by the business and written off to the statement of profit or loss.

**Option 3 Operating Lease**

Cost of Operating Lease

Annual lease rental payments £625,000

Monthly repayment is £625,000/12 = £52,083

Total cost is £1,250,000 over the 2 years

The lease term is not given and therefore the total costs are unknown. However as the asset is an operating lease it implies there is a useful economic life of the asset post lease term.

Advantages of Operating Lease

- Off balance sheet
- No effect to gearing or liquidity

Disadvantages of Operating Lease

- Possibility of paying for asset twice and therefore costs the business more
- No ownership of asset
- Commitment to make payments over lease term
- Risk and reward remains with lessor

Accounting Treatment

- The lease rental of £625,000 per annum will be charged to the statement of profit or loss.
- There will be no entries in the statement of financial position for the operating lease but has to be shown in a note detailing the non-cancellable annual commitments
- The operating lease is off balance sheet and the gearing will be unaffected.
- Therefore the total debt on the statement of financial position will be unaffected by the lease but a competent credit risk analyst will consider the size of the lease commitment and estimate a revised gearing position including the operating lease as finance.
- There will be no entry in current liabilities and the liquidity will be unaffected.

## INVESTING SURPLUS FUNDS

**133 D**

If £1 million is invested for one year at 7%, the value of the investment will be £1,000,000 × 1.07 = £1,070,000 after one year.

If £1 million is invested for three months at 6.5% per year and then for nine months at 7.5% per year, this means that the interest for the first three months will be 6.5% × 3/12 = 1.625%, and the interest for the next nine months will be 7.5% × 9/12 = 5.625%. The value of the investment after one year will therefore be:

£1,000,000 × 1.01625 × 1.05625 = £1,073,414.

This is £3,414 more than the income that would be obtained by investing at 7% for the full year.

However, there is a risk that interest rates will not rise during the first three months, and KIT will not be able to invest at 7.5% for the nine months, but only at a lower rate.

**134**

(a)     500,000 × 3% ÷ 12 × 10 = £12,500

(b)     500,000 × 5% ÷ 12 × 7 = £14,583

**135**   £100 × 5.3% ÷ £105 × 100 = 5.05%

**136**   Interest received = (150,000 × 6%) ÷ 2 = £4,500

Interest yield = 9,000 ÷ 175,000 × 100 = 5.14%

**137**   Annual interest = £800,000 × 4.5% = £36,000

Interest received = £36,000 ÷ 12 × 9 = £27,000

**138**   Three factors that would need to be considered when deciding how to invest short term cash surpluses are:

**Maturity**

A short term investment will involve investing the money for a specified period of time and receiving interest and the payment of the capital at a specified future date. The maturity date of the investment should be no longer than the duration of the cash surplus. If the cash is required before the maturity of the investment and the investment is 'cashed in' early, there will be the risk of loss of interest or capital value.

**Risk v Return**

Risk refers to the possibility that the investment might fall in value or that there may be some doubt about the eventual payment of interest or repayment of capital. Generally a higher risk investment will offer a higher return.

**Liquidity**

Liquidity refers to the ease with which an investment can be 'cashed in' without any significant loss of value or interest. All short-term investments are less liquid than cash in a bank current account, but some are more liquid than others. For example, many savings accounts or deposit accounts are reasonably liquid, as a depositor can withdraw cash immediately without penalty or for the loss of only several days' interest.

**139** £54,000 × 1.086^3 = £69164.50

**140** £20,000 × 1.034 = £20,680

**141** £2,500 ÷ 2 × 100 = £125,000

**142** Certificates of deposit are certificates issued by **banks** that certify that an amount of money has been deposited and will be repaid at a specific date in the future. They **can** be traded on a market. They are considered to be a **low risk** investment.

Local authority short-term loans are certificates issued by **local authorities** and backed by the government. They **can** be traded on a market. They are considered to be a **low risk investment**.

Government securities are also known as **gilt-edged** securities and **can** be traded. Interest rates are **fixed** and these types of securities are considered to be **low risk** because they **are** backed by the government.

Bank deposit accounts tend to have a **lower** return than shares, as they are much **lower** risk. They tend to have **lower** interest rates than gilts and debentures as they are a **more** liquid investment.

Shares are issued by **companies** and **can** be traded. Dividends are usually **variable**. Shares are considered to be a **high risk** investment. This is because the returns from shares are **sometime volatile** and the value of the investment is **uncertain.**

**143** Each £100 nominal value block gets 4% interest this is £4.00 cash.

To have received £600 interest we must have bought £600 ÷ £4 = 150 nominal value blocks

£9,000 was invested so market price = £9,000 ÷ 150 = £60

**144** £800,000 ÷ £0.50 = 1,600,000 shares

£640,000 ÷ 1,600,000 = £0.40

**145** £3 ÷ £30.50 × 100 = 9.84%

**146** 5,000 × £1.25 = £6,250

£6,250 + £700 = £7,000

£7,000 ÷ 5,000 = **£1.40**

**147**

| | Convertible within 45 days | Investment £20,000 or below | Interest rate 3% above base | Investment does not include shares | Low or Medium Risk |
|---|---|---|---|---|---|
| Option 1 | No | Yes | Yes | No | Yes |
| Option 2 | Yes | Yes | Yes | Yes | Yes |
| Option 3 | Yes | No | Yes | No | No |
| Option 4 | Yes | No | No | Yes | Yes |

The company should select **Option 2.**

**148** The returns given are over different time periods. It is necessary to calculate a rate per annum to enable the investments to be compared:

The annual return on the treasury bills is (£5/£995) × 365/91 = 2.02%

The annual return on the bank deposit account is 2.5%.

Treasury bills are generally considered risk free as they are guaranteed by the government of the country of issue. However during the present economic recession it has become evident that investment with countries that have previously been considered financially secure are not risk free. It should be borne in mind that the treasury bills are fixed dated and although they are negotiable this would incur costs and expose the company to price movement which will reflect the change in market interest rates. Although the return is fixed, if the company holds the bills for 91 days, market interest rates may rise with the result that the return on the treasury bills may be below market rates.

The deposit account has a variable interest rate which will introduce variability in the return, although this is likely to reflect market rates. Investments in banks are generally considered very low risk however after the world banking crisis in 2008/2009 it is now conceivable for a bank to fail. This introduces another albeit small element of risk in that there is liquidation risk of the bank itself. The deposit account lacks flexibility as it requires the company to give 30 days' notice of withdrawal or accept penalty interest charges.

The choice of investment will depend on the company's attitude to risk and whether they prefer to have a fixed return. The bank deposit account currently offers a higher return but may not continue to do so in the future.

**149** *Treasury bills*

Treasury bills reflect the credit rating of the country, so are generally low risk. The rate of interest is generally relatively low. In this case a yield of £10 would be earned over three months, which is an effective interest rate of only 1% per quarter.

*Equities*

The value of equities can go down as well as up. In this case, the equity index has increased for the last 14 months. However, this cannot be taken as a guarantee of future continued good performance. The equity index may fall rather than rise over the next few months.

The risk associated with a particular share depends upon the risk associated with the market in general and the risk associated with the particular company. In this case, the proposed companies are multinationals, which can result in a lower risk due to diversification. These companies pay an annual dividend but it may not be due during the investment period.

Due to the higher risk associated with equities, the yield is generally relatively high.

*Bank deposit*

A bank deposit is an investment in the business of the bank. However, banks are generally very secure, such that it is normally assumed that the investment will be recovered in full.

As with treasury bills, the yield is low to reflect the low risk, so carries a low rate of interest. However, in this case, the company would be required to give 30 days' notice of any withdrawals. This gives the bank more certainty and is reflected in an increased return on the deposit, in the form of an increased interest rate.

**150**

|  | Suitable options |
|---|---|
| A partnership has £50,000 to invest | Options 1, 2 and 3 |
| An investing organisation requires a low risk investment | Options 2 and 4 |
| A guaranteed interest rate of 3% is required | Options 3 and 4 |
| The notice period needs to be less than 50 days | Options 2, 3 and 4 |
| The investment should not include shares | Options 2 and 4 |

**151 Land**

- Historically land is deemed to be a fairly safe investment as there is a finite supply.

- However in the last decade land values have been volatile sometimes resulting in a capital loss for investors therefore it is now considered a high risk investment as the return is unknown.

- The initial investment of £250,000 may not be fully realised if the market value is lower than £250,000 at the date of sale.

- If the plan is to build on the land the planning permission will need to be sort. This will incur extra costs (e.g. legal, planning fees, advertising etc).

- Planning permission could be refused. This could have a negative impact on the value of the land. If planning permission is granted it could greatly increase the value of the land. It is unlikely that the return could be forecast with any certainty at the time of purchase.

- Land is usually seen as a long term investment and may take longer than three years to make a suitable return for the company.

- The investment can only be realised once the land is sold and the speed of this will depend upon the economic environment at the time of sale.

- The liquidity of the company may be adversely affected if they are unable to realise the full £250,000 at the end of three years.

**Long term bank deposit account**

- Investment in a bank deposit account is generally perceived to be a low risk option as the interest rate is fixed and a return is guaranteed.

- The return is likely to reflect the low risk and therefore be substantially less than could be earned on other investments. The initial investment is guaranteed.

- Traditionally bank deposit accounts were seen as risk free from the perspective of the loss of capital value. However in light of the global financial crisis there is a risk of loss of capital value if the deposit is not covered by a government backed guarantee scheme.

- The deposit account may have a minimum notice period to avoid early withdrawal however the funds could be available immediately, for a fee, if required even though the company would achieve a lower return than expected.

**Shares in public companies**

- Shares in public companies are generally perceived to be high risk because of market volatility and lack of control over business decisions made by those running the company.

- However high returns can be achieved with the right portfolio of shares held for a reasonable period of time.

- The company might spread the risk by selecting a portfolio which includes both low risk and high risk companies.

- The return achievable cannot be identified with any certainty at the time of investment.

- As shares can be sold at any point after purchase it would take only a few days for the company to realise its cash as long as it is prepared to take the price offered at that point in time.

- The company could also realise its cash piecemeal as and when required.

- The fees for buying and selling will need to be offset against any dividends and increase in share price when calculating the return.

**Certificates of deposit**

- A certificate of deposit (CD) is issued by a bank or building society which certifies that a certain sum, usually a minimum of £50,000, has been deposited with it to be repaid on a specific date.

- The term can range from seven days to five years but is usually for six months.

- CDs are negotiable instruments; they can be bought and sold, therefore if the holder does not want to wait until the maturity date the CD can be sold in the money market.

- CDs offer a good rate of interest and are highly marketable.

- CD is that they can be liquidated at any time at the current market rate. The market in CDs is large and active therefore they are an ideal method for investing large cash surpluses.

- The holder of the CD at maturity has the right to take the deposit with interest. CDs are negotiable instruments; they can be bought and sold, therefore if the holder does not want to wait until the maturity date the CD can be sold in the money market.

**Treasury bills**

- Treasury bills are negotiable instruments issued by the government, with a maturity of less than one year. In practice, most treasury bills have a maturity of three months (91 days). Cash is available for 3 years so this may not be the most suitable form of investment.

- Treasury bills are used by a government to finance short term cash requirements.

- Treasury bills are issued at regular intervals when investors are invited to apply to buy bills in the new issue.

- Since treasury bills are debts of the government, they have a high credit quality, risk is low, and yields for investors are therefore also lower than for many other short term investments. Treasury bills issued by a government and denominated in the domestic currency should be risk free.

- Treasury bills are redeemable at face value. Since the bills are redeemable at par, investors pay less than face value to buy them.

- Although yields on treasury bills are relatively low, they can be attractive short term investments because of their risk free nature and their liquidity. There is a large and active secondary market in treasury bills in the UK.

**152  Option 1**

- Fixed rate so a return is guaranteed

- The return is 6%

- Liquidity depends on the terms of the investment.  This option is a fixed term of 4 years.  It may be possible to redeem the investment early if the money is required but there is a risk of incurring early redemption charges/penalties, usually a couple of months interest but the capital amount is safe.

- Traditionally bank deposit accounts were seen as risk free from the perspective of the loss of capital value. However in light of the global financial crisis there is a risk of loss of capital value if the deposit is not covered by a government backed guarantee scheme.

- It may be possible to sell the bond before maturity

**Option 2**

- High risk investment

- The company may not be a listed FTSE100 company so selling the shares may be difficult affect the liquidity of this investment

- Share prices may increase but equally they could fall so the return is very uncertain

- A thorough investigation will need to be carried out on the company in question to analyse profits and profile.  Will dividends be paid?

- Helping this company to expand may well help the local area to improve by providing much needed employment which in turn may improve the image of the investing companies.  If it fails then this may have a negative impact on the investing companies

**Option 3**

- Very high risk investment

- Need to investigate the report regarding the abundance of oil as if the report is false the entire investment could be lost

- As with option 2 – it may be difficult to sell the shares if this company is not a listed company affecting liquidity

- A thorough investigation, including a site visit, will need to be carried out on the company in question to analyse profits and profile

- Ethical issues/damage to reputation for any investor if the claims of child labour and poor health and safety are true

**153**  (a)  $(1,500 \times 5\%) + (5,000 \times 8\%) + (1,000 \times 2.5\%) + (750 \times 1.2\%) = 75 + 400 + 25 + 9 = 509$

  $509 \div 8,250 \times 100 = \mathbf{6.2\%}$

  (b)  $509 - 25 = 484$

  $8,250 - 1,000 = 7,250$

  $484 \div 7250 \times 100 = 6.7\%$

**154**

**1. Current account**

- The amount of interest receivable on the current account is £4,000,000 × 0.4% = £16,000 per annum.
- 5-year return = £16,000 × 5 = £80,000
- Low risk
- Low return
- High liquidity

**2. Fixed rate account**

- The amount of interest receivable on the fixed rate account is £4,000,000 × 2.4% = £96,000 per annum.
- 5-year return £480,000
- Low risk
- High return (guaranteed)
- High liquidity – maybe penalties for early withdrawal

**3. Deposit account**

- The amount on interest receivable on the deposit account is £4,000,000 × 1.1% = £44,000 per annum.
- 5-year return £220,000
- Low risk
- Low return
- High liquidity – penalties for early withdrawal

**4. Treasury stock**

- The amount of interest receivable on the current account is £4,000,000 × 3% = £120,000 per annum.
- 5-year return £600,000
- Low risk
- High return
- High liquidity
- Issued by government
- Can be traded

**5. Certificates of deposit**

- The amount on interest receivable on the current account is £4,000,000 × 4% = £160,000 per annum.
- 5-year return £800,000
- Low risk
- High return
- High liquidity
- Issued by banks/building societies
- Can be traded
- Best return

**Recommendation**

The optimal solution, based purely on monetary values, is to invest in the certificates of deposit

*However, give marks if students mention that following recent banking disasters it may be more prudent to invest in the treasury stock as this is less risky.*

# Section 3

# MOCK ASSESSMENT QUESTIONS

**TASK 1** (8 marks)

M Jones owns a photographic business. The following forecast information has been produced.

The Statement of profit or loss for M Jones' business for the year ended December 20X5 is as follows:

|  | £ | £ |
|---|---|---|
| Revenue |  | 23,560 |
| Less: Purchases |  | (8,844) |
|  |  |  |
| Gross profit |  | 14,716 |
| Less: Expenses |  |  |
| Wages | 1,200 |  |
| Rent of darkroom | 2,000 |  |
| Postal charges | 1,760 |  |
| Printing expenses | 5,000 |  |
| Camera depreciation | 1,000 |  |
|  | ——— | (10,960) |
|  |  |  |
| Operating profit |  | 3,756 |

## Additional information

1 Photographic materials are purchased when required and therefore very little inventory is maintained.

2 All purchases are made on credit terms. The balance of trade payables at 1 January 20X5 was £2,240. Total payments for purchases during the year have been forecast as £8,824.

3 The balance of trade receivables at 1 January 20X5 was £2,480 and the company expects the trade receivables at 31 December to be equivalent of 10% of total sales for the year. M Jones believes that 95% of total sales will be on credit.

4 The statement of financial position shows an accrual for postal charges on £280 for the year ended 31 December 20X4. M Jones predicts that at the end of 20X5 there will be an accrual of £176 for postal charges.

5 There are also two prepayments showing for the year ended 31 December 20X4:

- Printing expenses £3,480

- Rent of darkroom £6,000

M Jones predicts that the closing prepayments for 20X5 will be:

- Printing expenses £2,268

- Rent of darkroom £6,000

6 The cash position at 1 January 20X5 was £500 in hand.

**Forecast the closing cash position at December 20X5.**

| | £ |
|---|---|
| Operating profit | |
| Change in trade receivables | |
| Change in trade payables | |
| Rent adjustment | |
| Postal charges adjustment | |
| Printing expenses adjustment | |
| Adjustments for non-cash items | |
| Net change in cash position | |
| Cash position 1 January 20X5 | |
| Forecast cash position 31 December 20X5 | |

## TASK 2 (8 marks)

M Jones is investigating the price of postage stamps over the last few years. The price for the last four years is given below.

**(a)** **Prepare an index for the price of postage stamps using 20X1 as the base period (to one decimal place).** **(2 marks)**

| Year | 20X1 | 20X2 | 20X3 | 20X4 |
|---|---|---|---|---|
| Price | 34p | 41p | 45p | 60p |
| Index | | | | |

M Jones uses the least squares regression line to forecast sales when he attends a wedding. The regression line has been identified as:

y = 100 + 50x

where y is the number of pictures sold and x is the number of guests in attendance.

M Jones will be attending the wedding of John and Mary who will have 350 guests in attendance.

**(b)** **Complete the following sentence.** **(2 marks)**

The forecast sales of pictures for John and Mary's wedding is_____

John and Mary's wedding is a summer wedding. M Jones always increases the sales volume by 5% for summer weddings.

**(c)** **Complete the following sentence.** **(2 marks)**

The adjusted forecast sales of pictures is_____

M Jones buys in photographic paper at £0.12 per sheet of 6" × 4" and he wishes to achieve a 20% margin or a 40% mark up.

**(d)** **Calculate the forecast selling price of the product** **(2 marks)**

The forecast selling price to achieve a 20% margin is £_____ (to the nearest penny)

The forecast selling price to achieve a 40% mark-up is £_____ (to the nearest penny)

## TASK 3 (10 marks)

The cash budget for M Jones for the three months ended March has been partially completed. The following information is to be incorporated and the cash budget completed.

- A bank loan of £5,000 has been negotiated and this will be paid into the business bank account in January. The loan term is 10 month beginning in February. Interest of 6% is added at the beginning of the loan term and the monthly repayments include both capital and interest elements.

- When M Jones uses its bank overdraft facility interest is payable monthly and is estimated at 2% of the previous months overdraft balance. The interest is to be rounded to the nearest £.

- M Jones needs to buy some new camera equipment costing £3,000. He has negotiated to pay for this in equal instalments over 3 months starting in February.

- At 1 January the balance of the bank account was £5,750.

**Using the information provided, complete the cash budget for M Jones for the three months ending March.**

Cash inflows should be entered as positive figures and cash outflows as negative figures. Zeroes must be entered where appropriate to achieve full marks.

|  | January £ | February £ | March £ |
|---|---|---|---|
| **RECEIPTS** | | | |
| Cash sales | 720 | 760 | 840 |
| Credit sales | 1,080 | 1,128 | 1,116 |
| Bank loan | | | |
| **Total receipts** | | | |
| **PAYMENTS** | | | |
| Purchases | −684 | −722 | −798 |
| Wages | −110 | −110 | −110 |
| Expenses | −2,200 | −2,200 | −2,200 |
| Capital expenditure | | | |
| Bank loan repayment | | | |
| Overdraft interest | | | |
| **Total payments** | | | |
| **Net cash flow** | | | |
| Opening bank balance | | | |
| Closing bank balance | | | |

**TASK 4** (10 marks)

A cash budget has been prepared for J Blacktusk and Co for the next four periods.

The budget was prepared based on the following sales volumes and a selling price of £12 per item.

|  | Period 1 | Period 2 | Period 3 | Period 4 |
|---|---|---|---|---|
| Sales volume (items) | 4,500 | 4,300 | 4,500 | 4,800 |

The pattern of cash receipts used in the budget assumed 20% of sales were received in the month of sale and the remaining 80% in the month following sale.

|  | Period 1 (£) | Period 2 (£) | Period 3 (£) | Period 4 (£) |
|---|---|---|---|---|
| Original forecast sales receipts | 10,800 | 53,520 | 52,080 | 54,720 |

J Blacktusk and Co are now considering offering a settlement discount of 2% for all credit sales settled in the period of sale. The pattern of sales receipts changes to 60% of sales received in the month of sale, 20% in the month following sale and the remaining 20% two months after sale.

**(a)** Complete the table below to calculate the sales receipts expected in periods 1 to 4:

(4 marks)

|  | Period 1 (£) | Period 2 (£) | Period 3 (£) | Period 4 (£) |
|---|---|---|---|---|
| Revised forecast sales receipts |  |  |  |  |

The company has managed to negotiate extended payment terms with its suppliers. The original budget was prepared on the basis of paying suppliers in the month following purchase. The revised payment terms allow for settlement of 30% in the month following purchase with the remaining payment two months after purchase.

The original budgeted purchase figures were:

|  | Period 1 (£) | Period 2 (£) | Period 3 (£) | Period 4 (£) |
|---|---|---|---|---|
| Purchases | 51,000 | 53,000 | 55,000 | 58,000 |

**(b)** Use the table below to calculate the expected purchase payments for periods 1 to 4

(4 marks)

|  | Period 1 (£) | Period 2 (£) | Period 3 (£) | Period 4 (£) |
|---|---|---|---|---|
| Revised timing of payments |  |  |  |  |

**(c)** Calculate how the revised receipts and payments will affect the cash flow for Blacktusk and Co.

(2 marks)

Blacktusk and Co will have £_____more/less cash at the end of Period 4.

**TASK 5** (12 marks)

The quarterly budgeted and actual figures for J Blacktusk and Co are provided below. A variance of more than 7% is considered to be significant.

| | Budgeted £ | Actual £ | Variance £ |
|---|---|---|---|
| Credit sales | 162,840 | 158,521 | 4,319 A |
| Cash sales | 95,325 | 95,847 | 522 F |
| Total receipts | 258,165 | 254,368 | |
| Credit purchases | 166,589 | 161,178 | 5,411 F |
| Cash purchases | 10,520 | 10,875 | 355 A |
| Capital expenditure | 12,000 | 20,000 | 8,000 A |
| Wages and salaries | 45,000 | 40,000 | 5,000 F |
| General expenses | 21,000 | 22,222 | 1,222 A |
| Total payments | 255,109 | 254,275 | |
| Net cash flow | 3,056 | 93 | |

**Produce a report that discusses how well cash flows have been managed for the quarter.**

## TASK 6 (32 marks)

**(a)** Why is liquidity management important? **(2 marks)**

A  Liquidity management is important to ensure that a company does not make a loss.

B  Liquidity management is important so that the shareholders can see how much return they will get on their investment.

C  Liquidity management is important so that the company can estimate how much cash is tied up in inventory and non-current assets.

D  Liquidity management is important so that the company can ensure that cash is available to discharge commitments.

**(b)** What are the two main ways that Governments use to control the supply of money, interest rates and the availability of credit? **(2 marks)**

|  | Tick |
|---|---|
| Fiscal policy |  |
| Taxation |  |
| Monetary policy |  |
| Quantitative easing |  |

**(c)** BDG has gathered the following information for the year ended 31 December 20X4

|  | 31 December 20X4<br>£000 |
|---|---|
| Gross profit | 800 |
| Trade receivables | 350 |
| Trade payables | 260 |
| Trade receivables collection period in days | 57.8 |
| Inventory holding period in days | 44.6 |

- 85% of sales are made on credit.
- 90% of purchases are on credit.
- Inventory as at 31st December 20X3 is £370,000.

Calculate the following to the nearest whole pound or day where relevant. **(8 marks)**

|  | £ or day |
|---|---|
| Sales revenue | £ |
| Cost of sales | £ |
| Inventories level in the statement of financial position | £ |
| Trade payables payment period in days | day |

**(d)** The cash operating cycle for BDG is ⬚ **days** **(2 marks)**

**(e)** If a business decreases its receivable days by 8 days and increases the inventory holding period by 5 days and increased the time it takes to pay its payables by 12 days, what is the impact on the cash operating cycle?

The cash operating cycle would increase/decrease by ⬚ days **(2 marks)**

**(f)** Tick the relevant box to complete each of the following sentences     **(2 marks)**

| | Too high | Too Low |
|---|---|---|
| Overtrading can occur when working capital levels are | | |
| Over-capitalisation can occur when working capital levels are | | |

**(g)** Which two of the following are signs of overtrading?     **(2 marks)**

A    Rapidly decreasing sales

B    Rapidly increasing sales

C    Increased profit margins

D    Short receivables collection periods

E    Longer payables payment periods

**(h)** What is the role of the treasury department in a trading company?     **(2 marks)**

| | Tick |
|---|---|
| Invest surplus funds | |
| Raise finance | |
| Reduce the tax liability | |
| To speculate on risky investments | |

**(i)** Which of the following best describes a variable rate of interest?     **(2 marks)**

A    Interest rate that is guaranteed not to exceed a specified level

B    Interest rate that remains the same for the period of borrowing

C    Interest charge that floats in line with bank base rates

D    Interest rate that fluctuates in line with an agreed indicator

**(j)** If an investment is low, what is the likely rate of return associated with it?     **(2 marks)**

| | Tick |
|---|---|
| Low return | |
| Medium return | |
| High return | |

**(k)** Tick if the following statements are true or false     **(4 marks)**

| Statement | True | False |
|---|---|---|
| Under the Bribery Act is in an offence to accept money as a reward for performing a relevant function improperly | | |
| Money laundering regulations cover accountants and solicitors | | |

**TASK 7** (22 marks)

(a) A company has a loan of £17,500 and an overdraft of £6,500. Shareholder funds amount to £25,000

**What is the gearing ratio?** (2 marks)

A 26.00%

B 48.98%

C 70.00%

D 142.86%

(b) A bank has offered to lend a company £80,000 to be repaid over 40 months in equal instalments. The flat rate of interest is 3.75% per annum.

**What is the monthly repayment of capital and interest to the nearest £?** (2 marks)

| £ |
|---|

(c) **What is the annual flat rate of interest for a loan of £800,000 over 10 years if the monthly repayments are £16,000?** (2 marks)

| %  |
|---|

(d) A company has arranged a bank overdraft facility of £40,000. It has the following terms:

- The current annual interest is 12.5%

- The interest is calculated on the closing monthly overdrawn balance and is included in the next month's opening balance

- Assume there are no differences in the monthly charges for the number of days in the month

**Calculate the monthly interest costs to the nearest penny. Minus signs must be used to denote any bank overdraft and interest to be paid** (10 marks)

|  | Month 3 | Month 4 | Month 5 | Month 6 | Month 7 |
|---|---|---|---|---|---|
| Forecast net cash flow | 17,500 | −17,500 | 25,000 | −25,000 | −20,000 |
| Opening balance | −15,000 |  |  |  |  |
| Closing balance before interest |  |  |  |  |  |
| Overdraft interest to be charged |  |  |  |  |  |

(e) **Identify if the following statement is true or false** (2 marks)

| Statement | True | False |
|---|---|---|
| A finance lease does not affect the gearing of a company |  |  |

(f)  **Which of the following best describes a capped rate of interest?**  (2 marks)

A  Interest rate that is guaranteed not to exceed a specified level

B  Interest rate that remains the same for the period of borrowing

C  Interest charge that floats in line with bank base rates

D  Interest rate that fluctuates in line with an agreed indicator

(g)  **Identify whether the following statements are true or false**  (2 marks)

| Statement | True | False |
|---|---|---|
| A fixed charge is security on a loan supplied by a group of assets | | |
| A floating charge is security on a loan supplied by a specific asset | | |

## TASK 8  (18 marks)

J Blacktusk and Co are planning to expand their production facilities. The expansion plans will require the purchase of new machinery at a cost of £80,000 and an average working capital increase of £35,000.

(a)  **Discuss the following possible options for raising the money.**

- Bank overdraft
- Bank loan
- Finance lease

(b)  **Suggest 2 other possible options that could be considered.**

(c)  **State which option(s) should be chosen.**

**TASK 9** (22 marks)

(a) A company has £1,000,000 to invest for 12 months.

The choices available are:

Option 1 - a deposit account offering interest at 10% per year, with interest paid quarterly

Option 2 - a deposit account offering interest at 10.25% per year, with interest paid annually

**Which deposit account gives the best return?** (2 marks)

| | Tick |
|---|---|
| Option 1 | |
| Option 2 | |

(b) **Identify if the following statement is true or false** (2 marks)

| Statement | True | False |
|---|---|---|
| A risk neutral investor will consider all options and will try and select one that maximises return | | |

(c) **Calculate the interest yield (to 2 decimal places) on 4.5% Treasury Stock 20X4 with a current market price of £125.** (2 marks)

The interest yield is_____%

(d) A company invests £35,000 in a 90 day notice period fixed interest deposit account for four years. The rate of interest is 7.5%.

**What is the balance in the account after four years if the interest is paid annually at the end of each year and the interest received remains in the account (to 2 decimal places)?**

£ (2 marks)

(e) A company invests £150,000 in shares of B Pearl, a quoted company. B Pearl has 2 million £1 shares in issue. The current market price of B Pearl's share is £1.25. B Pearl's operating profit in 20X3 was £0.7 million. The dividend paid to shareholders was 8p a share.

**What is the dividend yield for B Pearl?** (2 marks)

(f) A company is going to pay a dividend of £1.50 per share. The current market price is £15.50 per share.

**What is the dividend yield per share (2 decimal places)?** (2 marks)

(g) **Identify whether the following statements are true or false** (8 marks)

| Statement | True | False |
|---|---|---|
| Government securities are considered a low risk investment | | |
| Investing in land is considered to be a high risk investment | | |
| When inflation rises, interest rates generally increase | | |
| Gold is a type of commodity | | |

(h) A company has £576,000 invested in a one year fixed interest bond which pays 5% per annum. The company is going to have with draw the full amount from the investment in the 11th month of investment. The penalty for early redemption is the loss of one month's interest.

**Calculate the total amount of interest that the company will receive.** (2 marks)

**TASK 10** (18 marks)

Write a report which considers the risk, return and liquidity of the following investment options:

- Land
- Shares in a public company
- Gold

# Section 4

# ANSWERS TO MOCK ASSESSMENT QUESTIONS

## TASK 1

| | £ | Working |
|---|---|---|
| Operating profit | 3,756 | |
| Change in trade receivables | 124 | Opening = £2,480<br>Closing = £2,356 |
| Change in trade payables | 20 | Opening = £2,240<br>Closing = £2,240 + £8,844 − £8,824 = £2,260 |
| Rent adjustment | 0 | SOPL amount = £2,000<br>Cash paid = £6,000 +£2,000 − £6,000 = £2,000 |
| Postal charges adjustment | −104 | SOPL amount = £1,760<br>Cash paid = £280 + £1,760 − £176 = £1,864 |
| Printing expenses adjustment | 1,212 | SOPL amount = £5,000<br>Cash paid = £2,268 + £5,000 − £3,480 = £3,788 |
| Adjustments for other non-cash items | 1,000 | Depreciation |
| Net change in cash position | 6,008 | |
| Forecast cash position 1 January 20X5 | 500 | |
| Forecast cash position 31 December 20X5 | 6,508 | |

## TASK 2

(a)

| Year | 20X1 | 20X2 | 20X3 | 20X4 |
|---|---|---|---|---|
| Price | 34p | 41p | 45p | 60p |
| Index | | 120.6 | 132.4 | 176.5 |

(b)  The forecast sales of pictures for John and Mary's wedding is 17,600.

(c)  The adjusted forecast sales of pictures is 18,480.

(d)  The forecast selling price to achieve a 20% margin is £0.15 (to the nearest penny).

The forecast selling price to achieve a 40% mark-up is £0.17 (to the nearest penny).

**TASK 3**

|  | January £ | February £ | March £ |
|---|---|---|---|
| **RECEIPTS** |  |  |  |
| Cash sales | 720 | 760 | 840 |
| Credit sales | 1,080 | 1,128 | 1,116 |
| Bank loan | 5,000 | 0 | 0 |
| **Total receipts** | **6,800** | **1,888** | **1,956** |
| **PAYMENTS** |  |  |  |
| Purchases | −684 | −722 | −798 |
| Wages | −110 | −110 | −110 |
| Expenses | −2,200 | −2,200 | −2,200 |
| Capital expenditure | 0 | −1,000 | −1,000 |
| Bank loan repayment | 0 | −530 | −530 |
| Overdraft interest | 0 | 0 | 0 |
| **Total payments** | **−2,994** | **−4,562** | **−4,638** |
| **Net cash flow** | **3,806** | **−2,674** | **−2,682** |
| Opening bank balance | 5,750 | 9,556 | 6,882 |
| Closing bank balance | 9,556 | 6,882 | 4,200 |

**TASK 4**

(a)

|  | Period 1 (£) | Period 2 (£) | Period 3 (£) | Period 4 (£) |
|---|---|---|---|---|
| Period 1 sales | 31,752 | 10,800 | 10,800 |  |
| Period 2 sales |  | 30,341 | 10,320 | 10,320 |
| Period 3 sales |  |  | 31,752 | 10,800 |
| Period 4 sales |  |  |  | 33,869 |
| Period 5 sales |  |  |  |  |
| Revised forecast sales receipts | 31,752 | 41,141 | 52,872 | 54,989 |

(b)

|  | Period 1 (£) | Period 2 (£) | Period 3 (£) | Period 4 (£) |
|---|---|---|---|---|
| Revised timing of payments | 0 | 15,300 | 51,600 | 53,600 |

(c)    Blacktusk and Co will have £48,134 more cash at the end of Period 4

**Working:**

| Original total receipts | £171,120 | Revised total receipts | £180,754 |
|---|---|---|---|
| Original total payments | £159,000 | Revised total payments | £120,500 |
|  | ——— |  | ——— |
| Net cash flow | £12,120 |  | £60,254 |

**TASK 5**

**Capital expenditure (67% adverse)**

This is a very large percentage variance but is not a large sum of money if you consider the overall receipts (£254,368) and payments (£254,275) that occur within the business. It does still need to be investigated as a serious overspend has occurred with regards capital expenditure.

*Possible reasons*

Earlier expenditure may have been deferred to this period.

Prices may have increased since the budget was set.

The supplier may have reduced the availability of credit for capital purchases.

More assets or higher specification assets may have been purchased.

*Possible actions*

Future capital expenditure could be contracted for in advance with prices and payment terms agreed to avoid unexpected increases.

Capital expenditure could be deferred to a later period to avoid an adverse variance.

**Wages and salaries (11% favourable)**

*Possible reasons*

Less overtime may have been needed during the period.

There may have been a reduction in staff due to natural wastage or leavers which has reduced the payroll costs for the period.

The increase in capital expenditure may have been for machinery that has replaced employees.

*Possible actions*

If production levels have remained constant and have been accomplished without the need for overtime then identify any changes in production processes that have enabled this and continue for the future.

If the reduction is due to staff leaving which will need to be replaced then future budgets should not be reduced.

If the reduction is due to redundancies as staff are no longer required this could lead to further costs in redundancy packages but the efficiency of the machinery should level out the costs in the long run.

**TASK 6**

(a)    **D**

(b)

| | Tick |
|---|---|
| Fiscal policy | ✓ |
| Taxation | |
| Monetary policy | ✓ |
| Quantitative easing | |

(c)

| | Working | 31 December 20X4 £000 |
|---|---|---|
| Sales revenue | (350 ÷ 57.8 × 365) ÷ 85 × 100 | 2,600 |
| Cost of sales | 2,600 – 800 | 1,800 |
| Inventories level in the statement of financial position | 44.6 × 1,800 ÷ 365 | 220 |
| Trade payables payment period in days | 1,800 – (370 – 220) = 1,650 <br> 260 ÷ (0.90 × 1,650) × 365 | 63.9 days |

(d)  44.6 + 57.8 – 63.9 = 38.5 days

(e)  The cash operating cycle will decrease by 15 days – the decrease in the receivable days decreases the length of the cycle, the increase in inventory holding days increases the length of the cycle, the increase in the payment period decreases the length of the cycle – the net effect is a decrease of 15 days.

(f)

| | Too high | Too Low |
|---|---|---|
| Overtrading can occur when working capital levels are | | ✓ |
| Over-capitalisation can occur when working capital levels are | ✓ | |

(g)  **B and E**

(h)

| | Tick |
|---|---|
| Invest surplus funds | ✓ |
| Raise finance | ✓ |
| Reduce the tax liability | |
| To speculate on risky investments | |

(i)  **D**

(j)

| | Tick |
|---|---|
| Low return | ✓ |
| Medium return | |
| High return | |

(k)

| Statement | True | False |
|---|---|---|
| Under the Bribery Act is in an offence to accept money as a reward for performing a relevant function improperly | ✓ | |
| Money laundering regulations cover accountants and solicitors | ✓ | |

**TASK 7**

(a) **B**

(17,500 + 6,500) ÷ (17,500 + 6,500 + 25,000) × 100 = 48.98%

(b) **£2,250**

80,000 × 3.75% = £3,000 interest pa

£3,000 ÷ 12 × 40 = £10,000 total interest

(£80,000 + £10,000) ÷ 40 = £2,250

(c) **14%**

Total repayments = £16,000 × 12 × 10 = £1,920,000

Interest paid = £1,920,000 - £800,000 = £1,120,000

Interest rate = £1,120,000 ÷ £800,000 × 100 ÷ 10 years = 14%

(d)

|  | Month 3 | Month 4 | Month 5 | Month 6 | Month 7 |
|---|---|---|---|---|---|
| Forecast net cash flow | 17,500 | -17,500 | 25,000 | -25,000 | -20,000 |
| Opening balance | -15,000 | 2,500 | -15,156 | 9,844 | -15,314 |
| Closing balance before interest | 2,500 | -15,000 | 9,844 | -15,156 | -35,314 |
| Overdraft interest to be charged | 0 | -156 | 0 | -158 | -368 |

(e)

| Statement | True | False |
|---|---|---|
| A finance lease does not affect the gearing of a company |  | ✓ |

(f) **A**

(g)

| Statement | True | False |
|---|---|---|
| A fixed charge is security on a loan supplied by a group of assets |  | ✓ |
| A floating charge is security on a loan supplied by a specific asset |  | ✓ |

## TASK 8

(a)   **Bank overdraft**

A bank overdraft should not be relied upon for long term investments such as machinery. It would be possible to have discussions with the bank manager to see if it would be possible to have an overdraft that would cover the working capital increase of £35,000.

The reasons why a bank overdraft is not suitable for long term investments:

- The interest rate on an overdraft may be higher than that which could be negotiated on a loan. It is unlikely that the purchase cost of the machinery will be paid off in the short term; therefore the interest cost incurred by using an overdraft could be significant.

- An overdraft is 'repayable on demand'. The bank could cancel the overdraft facility and require any outstanding amount to be repaid, possibly causing severe cash flow repercussions for the business.

The reasons why a bank overdraft is suitable for funding the working capital:

- Overdraft interest is calculated on the value of the actual overdraft each day, and as the working capital amount may fluctuate, this would be the cheapest interest option.

- An overdraft can be flexible. Once the working capital requirement has been met, and the new machinery is fully operational and has increased cash flow, it will be possible to reduce the value of the overdraft.

Other points to note:

- Interest costs – these vary with base rates, making forecasting harder.

- Increasing the facility – once an overdraft facility has been agreed with the bank, it may be difficult to persuade the bank to increase that facility if additional finance is required.

- Security – the bank may require some form of security, either a fixed or a floating charge.

**Bank Loan**

A bank loan can be tailored to meet the requirements of the borrower. It can be taken out for a period which matches the assets which it is financing, and the repayment terms can be negotiated to match the cash flows from the asset or the other business cash flows.

*Advantages of a bank loan*

- Interest rates on loans tend to be lower than that on an overdraft.

- The source of finance is for an agreed term, so full repayment will not be demanded before the end of the agreement unless a number of repayments are missed.

*Disadvantages of a bank loan*

- If the interest on the loan is a fixed rate, then this is like to be more expensive than an overdraft or a variable rate loan. You will end up paying much more for the asset than it would have cost for cash. Interest is also calculated on the full amount of the loan, rather than daily as with an overdraft.

- The bank may impose certain restrictions or covenants, which will limit the freedom of action of the management of the business. For example, restrictions on payment of dividends or on other forms of finance taken out by the business.

**Finance lease**

Under a finance lease, the lessee has the use of the asset for most, if not all, of its useful life. All the risks and rewards are transferred to the lessee. The lessee will be responsible for the upkeep and maintenance of the asset and, to all intents and purposes, owns the asset. The finance lease charges will reflect the repayment of the value of the asset and the finance charge to the lessor.

*Advantages*

- The lessee may be able to sell the asset at the end of its life with only a proportion of the sale proceeds being returned to the lessor.
- Often an option to buy the asset at the end of the lease term.
- This may often be a cheaper form of financing the purchase of an asset than taking out a loan to purchase the asset outright.

*Disadvantages*

- Finance cost means that the price paid is more than the value of the asset.
- Asset is not owned at the end of the term of the lease.
- The lessee, although having use of the asset, never actually gains legal title to the asset.

(b) **Two other options** (choose from):

Hire purchase – purchase of an asset by instalments rather than cash includes an interest charge.

Operating lease – the asset is not treated as if it is owned, and lease payments are an expense.

Sale and operating leaseback – an asset is sold and the new owner leases it back. Cash is released in the sale.

Equity injection (selling shares) – shares could be sold to increase the equity or capital in the business. The advantage of these is that they do not have to be paid back.

Factoring – the sale of debts to a third party (the factor) at a discount in return for prompt cash. The debts of the company are effectively sold to a factor (normally owned by a bank). The factor takes on the responsibility of collecting the debt for an additional fee.

Invoice discounting – a third party advances cash and the receivables balance is used as security for the 'loan' of the cash.

(c) **Conclusion** (note any sensible and supported argument will gain marks):

Working capital – fund via bank overdraft or possibly factoring/invoice discounting.

Purchase of machinery – fund via loan, HP, operating lease or finance lease.

To make an informed decision further information would be required.

## TASK 9

(a)

| | Tick |
|---|---|
| Option 1 | ✓ |
| Option 2 | |

**Option 1**

10% interest per annum calculated quarterly means that interest is 2.5% a quarter for 4 quarters.

£1,000,000 × 1.025 = £1,025,000

£1,025,000 × 1.025 = £1,050,625

£1,050,625 × 1.025 = £1,076,891

£1,076,891 × 1.025 = £1,103,813

**Option 2**

£1,000,000 × 1.1025 = £1,102,500

Therefore Option 1 gives the better return

(b)

| Statement | True | False |
|---|---|---|
| A risk neutral investor will consider all options and will try and select one that maximises return | ✓ | |

(c)  £100 × 4.5% ÷ 125 × 100 = 3.6%

(d)  £35,000 × $1.075^4$ = £46,741.42

(e)  (8/125) × 100 = 6.4%

(f)  £1.50 ÷ £15.50 × 100 = 9.68%

(g)

| Statement | True | False |
|---|---|---|
| Government securities are considered a low risk investment | ✓ | |
| Investing in land is considered to be a high risk investment | ✓ | |
| When inflation rises, interest rates generally increase | ✓ | |
| Gold is a type of commodity | ✓ | |

(h)  £576,000 × 5% ÷ 12 × 10 = £24,000

## TASK 10

### Land

*Risk*

Land use to be considered as one of the most solid investments available as it will always be worth something, and there's little chance of it being stolen. However, in the last decade land values have been volatile, sometimes resulting in a capital loss for investors. Previous use of the land may mean that it is contaminated. Possible legislation issues such as agricultural ties or green belt regulations can limit what can be done to the land. There can be costly problems with getting planning permission. Therefore there is risk with regards the return available and also risk of losing the money invested.

*Return*

If planning permission is granted then land can be built on and sold or built on and rented out, increasing the value of the land. Purchase, maintenance and/or 'refurbishment' costs of the land can be high, reducing the possible profit on resale.

If planning permission is denied then it may be possible to rent the land as it is without development but this may reduce the value substantially.

If the market value is lower than the purchase price, at the date of sale, the initial investment may not be fully realised. It is unlikely that the return could be forecast with any certainty at the time of purchase.

*Liquidity*

The investment can only be realised once the land is sold and the speed of this will depend upon the economic environment at the time of sale.

### Shares

*Risk*

Shares in public companies are generally perceived to be high risk because of market volatility and lack of control over business decisions made by those running the company. The company could spread the risk by selecting a portfolio which includes both low risk and high risk companies.

*Return*

When you buy shares in a company you own part of that company and will receive a share of any profits by way of dividends. The best companies will find ways to increase revenue over and above the rate of inflation, or reduce costs, significantly increasing their profits. As the revenue increases, the value of each share should also rise, so, as well as a healthy level of income, you could also benefit from capital growth.

There are brokerage fees when shares are bought or sold, reducing the overall return, and share price fluctuation mean the return is uncertain. However, high returns can be achieved with the right portfolio of shares held for a reasonable period of time.

*Liquidity*

As shares can be sold at any point after purchase, it would take only a few days for the company to realise its cash, as long as it is prepared to take the price offered at that point in time. The company could also realise some of its cash as and when required.

**Gold**

*Risk*

Gold carries risk due to the fluctuations in value. Gold investment can be used at times when the markets are falling and when the inflation is very high, as the value of gold rises in times of high inflation.

*Return*

Gold, in any form, does not give an income, such as interest payments. The return achievable is not identifiable due to the fluctuations in price. Gold can be expensive to keep due to increased insurance and storage costs. There may also be broker charges.

*Liquidity*

Gold is very liquid; at any time gold can be converted to cash.